THE OFFICIAL
CorningWare®
MEAL MUG®
COOKBOOK

THE OFFICIAL
CorningWare®
MEAL MUG®
COOKBOOK

75 Easy Microwave Meals in Minutes

ROXANNE WYSS & KATHY MOORE

Robert
ROSE

For complete cataloging information, see page 170.

Disclaimer
The recipes in this book have been carefully tested by our kitchen and our tasters. To the best of our knowledge, they are safe and nutritious for ordinary use and users. For those people with food or other allergies, or who have special food requirements or health issues, please read the suggested contents of each recipe carefully and determine whether or not they may create a problem for you. All recipes are used at the risk of the consumer.

We cannot be responsible for any hazards, loss or damage that may occur as a result of any recipe use.

For those with special needs, allergies, requirements or health problems, in the event of any doubt, please contact your medical adviser prior to the use of any recipe.

At the time of publication, all URLs referenced link to existing websites. Robert Rose Inc. is not responsible for maintaining, and does not endorse the content of, any website or content not created by Robert Rose Inc.

COVER & BOOK DESIGN: Kevin Cockburn/PageWave Graphics Inc.

COVER & INTERIOR PHOTOGRAPHY: Brian Samuels

FOOD & PROP STYLING: Brian Samuels & Rebecca Arnold Saenz

EDITOR: Kathleen Fraser

INDEXER: Gillian Watts

Linen Background: © Getty Images

Published by Robert Rose Inc.
120 Eglinton Avenue East, Suite 800, Toronto, Ontario, Canada M4P 1E2
Tel: (416) 322-6552 Fax: (416) 322-6936
www.robertrose.ca

Printed and bound in Canada

1 2 3 4 5 6 7 8 9 MI 30 29 28 27 26 25 24 23 22

contents

INTRODUCTION

WHAT IS A MUG MEAL?

A quick, delicious mug meal is the answer when hunger pangs strike but time is precious, and when going out to eat is not convenient or possible. Whether at school or the office, working from home or just too busy to cook, everyday meals too often feature the same ole' cold fare. An appetizing, easy-to-prepare, warm mug meal is perfect for lunch, but is also ideal for breakfast on the run, when afternoon doldrums require a pick-me-up, or to satisfy late-night cravings.

The goal for each of these mouth-watering recipes was rapid microwave cooking, with few ingredients, in just a step or two. Your hot meal can be ready to enjoy in moments.

Best of all, many recipes have tips, so you can make it to go! Just fill the mug, pack with an ice pack, and know your meal will be hot and tasty and ready to eat in minutes.

SELECT THE MUG

Choose a microwave-safe mug that is the correct size. These recipes are all designed for a 20-oz (625 g) mug that is made from durable, microwave-safe stoneware. The best microwave-safe mug does not absorb food odors or flavors the way plastic cups can and it is dishwasher and freezer safe.

The CorningWare Meal Mug has a vented plastic lid that snaps on tightly for travel. The vent adds convenience so you can close the vent when traveling and open the vent for cooking. The plastic lid is BPA free and top-rack dishwasher safe. This mug does not heat up the way many plastic mugs can, it will not melt or warp from the heat, nor does it reflect microwave energy as cups with metallic trim or certain glazes might do.

FOR BEST RESULTS

Assemble the recipe in the mug as directed.

When cooking, follow the directions if food is to be covered. Some foods need to be covered to retain steam or prevent splattering, while other foods are cooked uncovered.

Always open the vent when cooking. Close the vent to seal the mug for food storage or travel.

Foods cooked in the microwave oven are often stirred midway through cooking, and some recipes rest after cooking.

Cook for the time suggested. Cooking times are estimates, so always heat the food until it is fully cooked. The cooking power for microwave ovens varies from about 600 to 1200 watts or more, and this affects the cooking time. Generally, the higher the cooking wattage, the more quickly it cooks. Once you use your microwave oven a time or two, you will be better able to predict if you should trim a few seconds off the recommended time or if an extra minute is needed to fully cook the food. You will also learn if the microwave oven you are using cooks food evenly or if the results are improved if you stir more often.

When cooking, the food and the steam will be hot. Use caution when opening the lid as the steam that escapes may burn. Likewise, the mug may become warm or even hot if cooking a soup or other recipe that cooks for several minutes. Use a hot-pad holder to carefully lift the hot mug.

If packing a mug meal for a child, make sure they know how to operate the microwave oven and can heat the food thoroughly and safely.

PLAN AHEAD

Plan ahead to prepare single-serving recipes in a snap.

When cooking pasta or browning ground beef or turkey, cook a little extra and spoon out a serving or two for future mug meals. Recipe-ready amounts of ¼ to 1 cup (60 to 250 mL) can be sealed in ziplock bags and refrigerated for up to three days or frozen for future use. To thaw, place frozen packages in the refrigerator overnight or use frozen when you assemble the mug recipe.

For canned beans, diced tomatoes, ready-to-use broth or jars of marinara sauce, use what is needed, then seal and refrigerate or freeze leftovers for future use.

Canned beans are an especially convenient, nutritious food. Use the amount needed for the recipe, then serve remaining beans in a salad, soup or casserole.

Frozen vegetables and fruits are readily available in loose-pack bags, so it is easy to measure out the needed volume.

Browse the grocery store for preprepared healthy foods. Quick cooking, microwave-ready items are increasingly popular, so there is a growing array of possibilities. Look for microwave-ready pasta, precooked rice, fully cooked sausage, chopped ham, rotisserie chicken and other foods that are convenient to use. Read labels carefully to identify if foods are processed with additives, heavily salted, or covered in sauces so you can avoid those and instead select foods that are more wholesome and nutritious.

Use the recipes in the book as a guide. If you cook a favorite large recipe of chili or soup, spoon some into the mug, filling about half-full. Cover, refrigerate and you have an individual serving of a meal ready to heat and enjoy. When reheating food, always microwave until it is steaming hot throughout.

MAKE IT TO GO

The main thing to remember is to keep it cold! When you are packing a meal to go, be sure to fill the mug with well-chilled food. Mug recipes take just minutes to assemble the night before or on a busy morning if ingredients are precooked and chilled.

If recipes include cooked meat, rice, pasta or other ingredients, precook the food the night before, then refrigerate until cold.

Pack the filled mug with ice packs in a backpack, thermal bag or lunch box. At the office or school, stash the mug in the refrigerator if available. Food safety is paramount. The food in the mug needs to stay well chilled until mealtime. The USDA recommends keeping foods cold, below 40°F (4°C), and any food stored at room temperature for 2 hours or more should be discarded.

Ingredients added in the second step or for serving should be packed separately in a sealed, travel-safe container or ziplock bag. Be sure to pack these perishable items with ice packs so they stay chilled until ready to eat.

breakfast

BACON EGG MUFFIN SANDWICH

No more paper bag stuffed with an assembly-line sandwich from the drive-through. This is the ideal quick recipe to make at home before you leave for the day. A hot breakfast sandwich is ready in a snap.

MAKES 1 SERVING | 1 (20 oz/625 g) microwave mug with vented cover

Nonstick cooking spray

2 large eggs

3 tbsp (45 mL) shredded Cheddar cheese

Salt and ground black pepper

1 English muffin, split and toasted

1 tsp (5 mL) unsalted butter, softened

2 slices precooked bacon

---

tip

You can omit the bacon and add a fully cooked turkey sausage patty. Or make the sandwich meatless by omitting the bacon altogether.

1 Spray mug with nonstick cooking spray. In prepared mug, whisk eggs. Stir in cheese and season to taste with salt and pepper.

2 Microwave, uncovered, on High for 1 minute. Stir and continue to microwave, uncovered, on High for 45 seconds.

3 Spread each piece of the English muffin lightly with butter.

4 Scoop cooked egg onto the bottom half of muffin. Fold bacon strips in half to fit on egg, then top with second half of the muffin. Serve warm.

BREAKFAST BURRITO

Some days you need a filling breakfast, yet still need to get out the door fast. This breakfast burrito has become a morning staple in our home.

MAKES 1 SERVING | 1 (20 oz/625 g) microwave mug with vented cover

Nonstick cooking spray

1 6-inch (15 cm) flour tortilla

2 large eggs, beaten

3 tbsp (45 mL) crumbled cooked sausage

2 tbsp (30 mL) shredded Cheddar cheese

1 tbsp (15 mL) salsa

Salsa, sour cream and chopped green onion (optional)

---

tip

You can substitute cooked bacon or ham for the sausage or leave the meat out altogether.

1 Spray the mug with nonstick cooking spray. Line prepared mug with tortilla, forming a bowl in the center.

2 In a small bowl, combine eggs, sausage, cheese and salsa. Pour egg mixture into tortilla bowl. Microwave, uncovered, on High for 2 minutes. Stir and continue to microwave, uncovered, on High, for 1 minute.

3 Let stand, covered, for 1 minute. Enjoy straight from the mug or run a knife around the edge to loosen and place the burrito bowl on a plate. Garnish with salsa, sour cream and chopped green onion (if using).

MAKE IT TO GO

Place tortilla in a ziplock bag. Spray the mug with nonstick cooking spray. Combine egg, sausage, cheese and salsa in mug as directed in Step 2. Cover mug, close vent and pack with ice packs. When ready to eat, open vent and microwave as directed in Step 2. Warm tortilla separately in the microwave oven, then spoon egg mixture into the tortilla.

CRUSTLESS QUICHE

There is no need for a crust in this delicious quiche. This recipe calls for chopped broccoli and Swiss cheese, but you can customize the flavor as you prefer. Chopped spinach or kale would be delicious in place of the broccoli, while Cheddar or Colby-Jack cheese are great substitutes for the Swiss cheese.

MAKES 1 SERVING | 1 (20 oz/625 g) microwave mug with vented cover

Nonstick cooking spray

2 large eggs

1/3 cup (75 mL) half-and-half (10%) cream

1/2 tsp (2 mL) Dijon mustard

Salt and ground black pepper

1/2 cup (125 mL) frozen chopped broccoli, thawed and drained

1/2 cup (125 mL) shredded Swiss cheese

1 Spray the mug with nonstick cooking spray.

2 In the mug, whisk together the eggs, cream and Dijon. Season to taste with salt and pepper. Stir in the broccoli and cheese.

3 Microwave, uncovered, on High for 1 minute. Stir and continue to microwave on High, uncovered, for 1 1/2 to 2 minutes. Let rest 1 minute.

MAKE IT TO GO

Follow directions through Steps 1 and 2. Cover mug, close vent and pack with ice packs. When ready to eat, open vent and continue as directed in Step 3.

SAUSAGE, KALE AND CHEDDAR FRITTATA

A frittata is an Italian omelet that uses up whatever ingredients you have on hand. Here, the eggs are mixed with meat, vegetables and cheese. This recipe is ideal for busy mornings; enjoy it at home or Make It To Go when you need breakfast on the run.

MAKES 1 SERVING | 1 (20 oz/625 g) microwave mug with vented cover

Nonstick cooking spray

2 large eggs

Salt and ground black pepper

$\frac{1}{3}$ cup (75 mL) frozen chopped kale

$\frac{1}{4}$ cup (60 mL) crumbled cooked pork sausage or turkey sausage

2 tbsp (30 mL) shredded sharp (old) Cheddar cheese

1 Spray the mug with nonstick cooking spray.

2 In the mug, whisk together eggs, salt and pepper. Stir in kale, sausage and cheese.

3 Microwave, uncovered, on High for 1 minute. Stir and continue to microwave, uncovered, for $1\frac{1}{2}$ to 2 minutes. Let rest 1 minute.

tip

You can substitute cooked bacon or ham for the sausage or omit the meat, if you prefer.

MAKE IT TO GO

Follow directions through Steps 1 and 2. Cover mug, close vent and pack with ice packs. When ready to eat, open vent and continue as directed in Step 3.

BISCUIT WITH SAUSAGE GRAVY

How do you spell early-morning comfort? Biscuits and gravy, of course! Many a day this has also been called dinner at our home. Keep biscuits in the freezer so when the urge strikes you are ready to make a breakfast treat that will stick with you until lunch.

MAKES 1 SERVING | 1 (20 oz/625 g) microwave mug with vented cover

½ cup (125 mL) crumbled cooked pork sausage or turkey sausage

1 tbsp (15 mL) butter, cut into small cubes

1½ tbsp (22 mL) all-purpose flour

Salt and ground black pepper

¾ cup (175 mL) milk

1 large baked biscuit or 2 small baked biscuits

tip

Keep bags of cooked, frozen sausage in the freezer for easy and fast prep, or purchase fully cooked turkey sausage crumbles in a bag and measure out what you need.

1 In the mug, combine sausage and butter. Microwave, uncovered, on High for 30 seconds. Stir well.

2 Stir in flour. Season to taste with salt and pepper. Gradually stir in milk and stir to combine. Microwave, uncovered, on High for 1½ minutes. Stir and continue to microwave, uncovered, on High for an additional 1½ minutes.

3 Break biscuit into bite-size pieces and gently stir into the gravy or slice biscuit in half and place on a plate, then ladle gravy over top.

MAKE IT TO GO

Place sausage and butter in the mug as directed in Step 1, but do not microwave. Cover mug, close vent and pack with ice packs. Pack flour, salt and pepper together in a container or ziplock bag. Pack milk in a sealed travel-safe container and pack with ice packs. Place biscuit in a ziplock bag. When ready to eat, continue as directed in Step 1.

BERRY FRENCH TOAST

While the look may not be the same as full slices of French toast arranged on a platter, all of the flavor is still captured in this easy mug version of the classic favorite.

MAKES 1 SERVING | 1 (20 oz/625 g) microwave mug with vented cover

3 slices French baguette bread (about ¾-inch/2 cm thick)

1 tsp (5 mL) butter, softened

¼ cup (60 mL) dried blueberries or dried mixed berries

1 large egg

3 tbsp (45 mL) milk

1 tbsp (15 mL) maple syrup

Maple syrup or confectioners' (icing) sugar, sifted (optional)

1 Lightly spread one side of each slice of bread with butter. Cut the slices into ¾-inch (2 cm) cubes. In the mug, combine bread cubes and dried berries.

2 In a small bowl, whisk together egg, milk and maple syrup. Pour egg mixture over the bread. Gently stir to coat the bread with the egg mixture.

3 Microwave, uncovered, on High for 1½ minutes. Let rest 1 minute.

4 To serve, drizzle with additional maple syrup or dust with confectioners' sugar, if using.

tips

Any firm, crusty bread will be delicious in the French toast. Soft white bread is not recommended. You should have about 1 cup (250 mL) of bread cubes.

If desired, omit the dried berries. Add ¼ tsp (1 mL) ground cinnamon to the egg and milk mixture. Proceed as the recipe directs. Garnish with fresh berries, if desired.

MAKE IT TO GO

Combine ingredients in the mug as directed in Step 1. Cover mug, close vent and pack. Combine eggs, milk and syrup in a sealed, travel-safe container and pack with ice packs. Place additional maple syrup in a small sealed, travel-safe container or place confectioners' sugar in a ziplock bag. When ready to eat, proceed as directed in Step 2.

MAPLE MUESLI WITH APPLES AND PECANS

We've taken muesli, a delicious mixture of cereals, and added dried apples and pecans, then sweetened the mix with a touch of maple syrup. When the muesli is served hot with milk, the result is a warm, hearty, nutritious breakfast. Make it the night before, refrigerate overnight and in the morning just pop it into the microwave oven. Nothing could be easier.

MAKES 1 SERVING | 1 (20 oz/625 g) microwave mug with vented cover

1/3 cup (75 mL) large-flake (old-fashioned) rolled oats

2 tbsp (30 mL) chopped pecans

2 tbsp (30 mL) chopped dried apples

1 tbsp (15 mL) wheat germ

1 tbsp (15 mL) raw sunflower seeds

1 tbsp (15 mL) maple syrup

2/3 cup (150 mL) milk or almond milk

1 In the mug, combine oats, pecans, apples, wheat germ, sunflower seeds and maple syrup. Stir in milk. Cover and refrigerate overnight, or about 12 hours.

2 Microwave, covered, on High for 1 minute. Stir and continue to microwave, covered, on High for 30 seconds. Let rest 1 minute.

MAKE IT TO GO

Combine ingredients in the mug as directed in Step 1. Cover mug, close vent and pack with ice packs. When ready to eat, open vent and continue as directed in Step 2.

CRANBERRY PECAN OATMEAL

You don't need to wait for cold weather to enjoy a bowl of cranberry-studded oatmeal. This healthy breakfast is satisfying no matter what the weather forecast. Get a good night's sleep filled with sweet dreams, knowing that breakfast can be prepared in a matter of minutes.

MAKES 1 SERVING | 1 (20 oz/625 g) microwave mug with vented cover

⅔ cup (150 mL) milk or unsweetened almond milk

½ cup (125 mL) large-flake (old-fashioned) rolled oats

2 tbsp (30 mL) dried sweetened cranberries

⅛ tsp (0.5 mL) salt

1 tbsp (15 mL) packed dark brown sugar

1 tbsp (15 mL) toasted chopped pecans

1 In the mug, combine milk, oats, cranberries and salt.

2 Microwave, uncovered, on High for 2 minutes. Let stand for 2 minutes. Stir in brown sugar and sprinkle with pecans.

MAKE IT TO GO

Combine milk and salt in the mug. Cover mug, close vent and pack with ice packs. Pack oats and cranberries in a ziplock bag. Pack brown sugar and pecans in a separate ziplock bag. When ready to eat, uncover mug and stir in oats and cranberries. Continue as directed in Step 2.

tip

Toasting pecans intensifies the flavor. Spread chopped pecans in a single layer on a baking sheet. Bake at 350°F (180°C) for 5 to 7 minutes or until lightly toasted. Cool and use as directed in the recipe.

variation

Raisin and Cinnamon Pecan Oatmeal: Omit dried cranberries and substitute raisins. Add ½ tsp (2 mL) ground cinnamon with raisins and stir well. Proceed as directed in Step 1.

soups and chilies

MARINARA MEATBALL SOUP

This soup combines tender meatballs, vegetables and pasta in a marinara-type broth. Garlic toast makes a perfect companion to this soup. The flavor combination will have you counting the minutes until lunch.

MAKES 1 SERVING | 1 (20 oz/625 g) microwave mug with vented lid

1 cup (250 mL) marinara or spaghetti sauce

½ cup (125 mL) ready-to-use beef broth

2 or 3 frozen, fully cooked meatballs

2 tbsp (30 mL) finely chopped celery

1 tbsp (15 mL) finely chopped carrot

1 tbsp (15 mL) dry minced onion

¼ tsp (2 mL) dried Italian seasoning

½ cup (125 mL) cooked ditalini pasta or other small pasta

Shredded Parmesan cheese (optional)

tip

If using meatballs that have been thawed, you can reduce the microwave time to 1 to 2 minutes, covered on High after adding the pasta.

1 In the mug, combine marinara sauce, broth, meatballs, celery, carrots, onion and Italian seasoning. Stir well.

2 Microwave, covered, on High for 2½ to 3 minutes. Add cooked pasta and stir well. Microwave, covered, on High for 2½ to 3 minutes. Sprinkle with Parmesan (if using).

MAKE IT TO GO

Combine the ingredients in the mug as directed in Step 1. Cover mug, close vent and pack with ice packs. Pack cooked pasta and Parmesan in separate containers or ziplock bags with ice packs. When ready to eat, open vent and continue as directed in Step 2.

CHICKEN TORTILLA SOUP

This is a great version of what has become a mainstay in many households. The star ingredient is the lime juice, as it adds just the right pop and depth of flavor to make this a favorite.

MAKES 1 SERVING | 1 (20 oz/625 g) microwave mug with vented cover

1 cup (250 mL) ready-to-use chicken broth

1 cup (250 mL) canned diced tomatoes with juice

1/2 cup (125 mL) chopped cooked chicken

2 tbsp (30 mL) minced fresh cilantro

1 tbsp (15 mL) freshly squeezed lime juice

1 tbsp (15 mL) dry minced onion

1/2 tsp (2 mL) chili powder

1/2 tsp (2 mL) ground cumin

1/4 tsp (1 mL) dry minced garlic

4 tortilla chips, crushed

1 tbsp (15 mL) shredded Cheddar cheese

1 In the mug, combine broth, tomatoes, chicken, cilantro, lime juice, onion, chili powder, cumin and garlic.

2 Microwave, uncovered, on High for 2 minutes. Stir and continue to microwave, uncovered, on High for 2 to 2 1/2 minutes. Top with tortilla chips and cheese.

MAKE IT TO GO

Combine ingredients in the mug as directed in Step 1. Cover mug, close vent and pack with ice packs. Pack chips and cheese in separate containers or ziplock bags. When ready to eat, uncover and continue as directed in Step 2.

EASY VEGETABLE SOUP WITH PASTA

Let those cold winter winds blow, and stay snug inside. This delicious soup will chase away the chill.

MAKES 1 SERVING | 1 (20 oz/625 g) microwave mug with vented cover

¾ cup (175 mL) frozen mixed vegetables

¼ cup (60 mL) crumbled cooked ground beef or ground turkey (optional)

⅓ cup (75 mL) cooked small shell pasta

1 cup (250 mL) vegetable juice cocktail or tomato juice

½ tsp (2 mL) dried Italian seasoning

Salt and ground black pepper

tip

To make this soup quick to prepare, store cooked ground beef and cooked pasta in premeasured small ziplock bags in the freezer. If meat and pasta are frozen, increase cooking time by about 1 minute or until soup is hot.

1 In the mug, combine vegetables, beef (if using) and pasta. Stir in the juice and Italian seasoning. Season to taste with salt and pepper.

2 Microwave, covered, on High for 3½ to 4 minutes. Let rest 1 minute. Stir.

MAKE IT TO GO

Combine ingredients in the mug as directed in Step 1. Cover mug, close vent and pack with ice packs. When ready to eat, open vent and continue as directed in Step 2. If vegetables are thawed, reduce cooking time to 3 minutes.

TOMATO SOUP

Tomato soup is everyone's favorite. This mug version is quick, easy to assemble and tastes delicious. If you desire a creamy soup, stir in cream just before serving.

MAKES 1 SERVING | 1 (20 oz/625 g) microwave mug with vented cover

1 cup (250 mL) crushed tomatoes or tomato purée

¼ cup (60 mL) ready-to-use chicken or vegetable broth

½ tsp (2 mL) granulated sugar

¼ tsp (1 mL) dried basil leaves

Salt and ground black pepper

1 tbsp (15 mL) half and half (10%) cream, heavy or whipping (35%) cream, or milk (optional)

1 In the mug, combine tomatoes, broth, sugar and basil. Season to taste with salt and pepper.

2 Microwave, covered, on High for 1½ to 2 minutes. Stir in cream or milk (if using).

tip

Who doesn't enjoy a grilled cheese sandwich with tomato soup? While a hot grilled cheese sandwich may be difficult to serve if you make this soup to go, you can easily add a little crunch and a hint of cheese flavor. Pack croutons (preferably those that are cheese- and herb-flavored), cheese crisps or cheese crackers in a ziplock bag. Just before serving, top the soup with croutons or serve the crisps or crackers alongside.

MAKE IT TO GO

Combine ingredients in the mug as directed in Step 1. Cover mug, close vent and pack with ice packs. Pack half and half (10%) cream, heavy or whipping (35%) cream, or milk (if using) in a sealed, travel-safe container with ice packs. When ready to eat, open vent and continue as directed in Step 2.

CHICKEN AND RICE SOUP

This soul-satisfying, brothy soup is one of our top three soup mug recipes. In sickness and in health, this soup is sure to please. It is perfect for using up leftover chicken or frozen cooked chicken. Try it with a spoonful of oyster crackers stirred in just before serving.

MAKES 1 SERVING | 1 (20 oz/625 g) microwave mug with vented cover

½ cup (125 mL) chopped cooked chicken

2 tbsp (30 mL) uncooked instant white rice

2 tbsp (30 mL) shredded carrots

1 tsp (5 mL) dried parsley flakes

½ tsp (2 mL) dry minced onion

Salt and ground black pepper

¾ cup (175 mL) ready-to-use chicken broth

1 In the mug, combine chicken, rice, carrots, parsley flakes and onion. Season to taste with salt and pepper. Stir in chicken broth.

2 Microwave, uncovered, on High for 2½ to 3 minutes. Remove from the microwave. Cover the mug, close vent and let rest 5 minutes.

tip

If you don't have chicken broth on hand, substitute 1 tsp (5 mL) chicken bouillon granules and ¾ cup (175 mL) water for the broth.

GINGER CHICKEN SOUP WITH CABBAGE AND WONTONS

Super-fast but still packed with the flavors of a carry-out soup from your favorite, neighborhood restaurant. Look for packages of cole slaw mix in the produce aisle to use instead of slicing cabbage.

MAKES 1 SERVING | 1 (20 oz/625 g) microwave mug with vented cover

$1\frac{1}{3}$ cups (325 mL) ready-to-use chicken broth

$\frac{1}{2}$ cup (125 mL) coleslaw mix

$\frac{1}{4}$ cup (60 mL) chopped cooked chicken

1 tbsp (15 mL) soy sauce

1 green onion, thinly sliced

$\frac{1}{8}$ tsp (0.5 mL) garlic powder

$\frac{1}{8}$ tsp (0.5 mL) ground ginger

Ground black pepper

3 wonton wrappers ($3\frac{1}{2}$-inch/8.5 cm squares) sliced $\frac{1}{2}$-inch/1 cm thick

1 In the mug, combine broth, coleslaw, chicken, soy sauce, green onion, garlic powder and ginger. Season to taste with pepper.

2 Microwave, covered, on High for 3 to $3\frac{1}{2}$ minutes. Lift and separate the cut wonton strips, then stir strips gradually into hot soup. Continue to microwave, covered, for 20 to 30 seconds. Let rest 1 minute.

MAKE IT TO GO

Combine ingredients in the mug as directed in Step 1. Cover the mug, close vent and pack with ice packs. Pack wonton strips in a ziplock bag. When ready to eat, open vent and continue as directed in Step 2.

BROCCOLI CHEESE SOUP

While this delicious soup may remind you of a favorite restaurant meal, you no longer have to go out for lunch. Just combine a few simple ingredients and know that a tasty and nutritious lunch will be ready for you.

MAKES 1 SERVING | 1 (20 oz/625 g) microwave mug with vented cover

¼ cup (60 mL) frozen chopped broccoli

1 tsp (5 mL) cornstarch

½ tsp (2 mL) dry minced onion

¼ tsp (1 mL) salt

¼ tsp (1 mL) ground black pepper

⅔ cup (150 mL) half and half (10%) cream

½ cup (125 mL) shredded Cheddar cheese

1 Place broccoli, cornstarch, onion, salt and pepper in the mug. Stir well. Stir in cream and cheese.

2 Microwave, covered, on High for 1½ minutes. Let stand, covered, for 1 minute. Stir well.

MAKE IT TO GO

Combine the ingredients in the mug as directed in Step 1. Cover mug, close vent and pack with ice packs. When ready to eat, open the vent and continue as directed in Step 2.

COUNTRY POTATO SOUP

Refrigerated diced potatoes, found in the dairy section at the grocery store, usually near the eggs, make this soup a snap to prepare. No need to spend extra time boiling and dicing the potatoes.

MAKES 1 SERVING | 1 (20 oz/625 g) microwave mug with vented cover

¼ cup (60 mL) finely chopped celery

1 tbsp (15 mL) butter, cut into small cubes

2 tsp (10 mL) dry minced onion

1 tbsp (15 mL) all-purpose flour

1 cup (250 mL) milk

1 cup (250 mL) diced, refrigerated hash brown potatoes

Salt and ground black pepper

¼ cup (60 mL) shredded Cheddar cheese

1 slice bacon, cooked and crumbled (optional)

1 In the mug, combine celery, butter and onion.

2 Microwave, covered, on High for 2 minutes.

3 Stir in flour. Gradually stir in milk. Add potatoes. Season to taste with salt and pepper. Microwave, covered, on High for 2 minutes.

4 Stir in cheese. Continue to microwave on High, uncovered, for 1½ minutes. Sprinkle with bacon (if using).

tip

Substitute cooked, diced potatoes in place of the store-bought refrigerated variety.

MAKE IT TO GO

Combine celery, butter and onion in the mug as directed in Step 1. Cover mug, close vent and pack with ice packs. Pack milk in a small sealed travel-safe container with ice packs. Pack flour, potatoes, salt, pepper, cheese and bacon (if using) in separate containers or ziplock bags with ice packs. When ready to eat, open vent and continue as directed in Step 2.

SWEET POTATO AND BLACK BEAN SOUP

Two super nutritious foods, the sweet potato and beans, combine in this low-fat soup. Add splendid flavor and quick-to-fix to that list and this soup is a winner.

MAKES 1 SERVING | 1 (20 oz/625 g) microwave mug with vented cover

1 cup (250 mL) frozen cubed sweet potatoes

1/2 cup (125 mL) canned black beans, drained and rinsed

1 tsp (5 mL) dry minced onion

1 tsp (5 mL) chili powder

Salt and ground black pepper

2/3 cup (150 mL) tomato juice

1/4 cup (60 mL) ready-to-use beef broth

1 In the mug, combine sweet potatoes, beans, onion and chili powder. Season to taste with salt and pepper. Pour juice and broth over vegetables.

2 Microwave, covered, on High for 4 minutes.

MAKE IT TO GO

Combine ingredients in the mug as directed in Step 1. Cover mug, close vent and pack with ice packs. When ready to eat, open vent and continue as directed in Step 2. If potatoes are thawed, reduce cooking time to 2 1/2 to 3 minutes.

tips

Do you have leftover roasted sweet potatoes? Substitute cubes of the roasted, peeled sweet potato for the frozen potatoes. Reduce cooking time to 2 1/2 to 3 minutes.

Individual cans or bottles of juice are a convenient way to keep juice on hand without worry of waste. A 5.5-oz/163 mL can of tomato juice measures 2/3 cup (150 mL) and is exactly what you need for this recipe.

CHICKEN CORN CHOWDER

Corn, chicken and bacon combine to make a hearty, tasty soup that will satisfy on any cool day.

MAKES 1 SERVING | 1 (20 oz/625 g) microwave mug with vented cover

¾ cup (175 mL) frozen corn

½ cup (125 mL) chopped cooked chicken

¼ cup (60 mL) frozen hash brown potatoes (diced or Southern style, preferred)

1½ tsp (7 mL) dry minced onion

1 slice bacon, cooked and crumbled

Salt and ground black pepper

⅔ cup (150 mL) ready-to-use chicken broth

1 In the mug, combine corn, chicken, potatoes, onion and bacon. Season to taste with salt and pepper. Pour broth over all.

2 Microwave, covered, on High for 4 minutes.

MAKE IT TO GO

Combine ingredients in the mug as directed in Step 1. Cover mug, close vent and pack with ice packs. When ready to eat, open vent and continue as directed in Step 2. If vegetables are thawed, reduce the cooking time to 3 to 3½ minutes.

TACO SOUP

While handheld tacos are delicious, they can be messy to eat. This taco soup has all the flavor of a taco and it is easy to enjoy at your desk or at home.

MAKES 1 SERVING | 1 (20 oz/625 g) microwave must with vented cover

½ cup (125 mL) crumbled cooked ground beef

½ cup (125 mL) canned diced tomatoes with juice

½ cup (125 mL) fresh or frozen corn

½ cup (125 mL) canned black beans, drained and rinsed

2 tsp (10 mL) dry minced onion

1 tsp (5 mL) chili powder

½ tsp (2 mL) ground cumin

½ tsp (2 mL) garlic powder

⅓ cup (75 mL) crushed tortilla chips

Sour cream, shredded Cheddar cheese, and diced green onion (optional)

1 In the mug, combine ground beef, tomatoes, corn, beans, onion, chili powder, cumin and garlic powder.

2 Microwave, covered, on High for 1½ minutes. Stir and continue to microwave, covered, on High for 2 minutes. Place the tortilla chips on top. Garnish with sour cream, cheese and green onion (if using).

tips

Brown the ground beef the night before and refrigerate it overnight. In the morning you can quickly combine the chilled beef with remaining ingredients.

Omit chili powder, cumin and garlic powder. Use 2 tsp (10 mL) taco seasoning mix instead.

Pinto beans or kidney beans can be substituted for the black beans.

MAKE IT TO GO

Combine ingredients in the mug as directed in Step 1. Cover mug, close vent and pack with ice packs. Pack tortilla chips, cheese and green onion in separate containers or ziplock bags with ice packs. Pack sour cream in a small, sealed, travel-safe container with ice packs. When ready to eat, open vent and continue as directed in Step 2.

EASY CHICKEN POSOLE

Posole, a light pork or chicken stew, contains hominy. Hominy is a dried variety of corn with large kernels that adds a chewy, robust flavor to this soup. Lime juice and cilantro complete the flavors.

MAKES 1 SERVING | 1 (20 oz/625 g) microwave mug with vented cover

1 tbsp (15 mL) butter, cut into small cubes

2 tsp (10 mL) dry minced onion

2 tsp (10 mL) all-purpose flour

½ tsp (2 mL) chili powder

½ tsp (2 mL) ground cumin

¼ tsp (1 mL) garlic powder

Salt and ground black pepper

1¼ cups (310 mL) ready-to-use chicken broth

½ cup (125 mL) chopped cooked chicken

½ cup (125 mL) canned white hominy, drained

1 tbsp (15 mL) canned chopped green chilies, drained

1 tbsp (15 mL) chopped fresh cilantro

2 tsp (10 mL) freshly squeezed lime juice

1 tbsp (15 mL) crisp tortilla strips

1 In the mug, stir together butter, onion, flour, chili powder, cumin, and garlic powder. Season to taste with salt and pepper. Add the chicken broth, chicken, hominy and green chilies.

2 Microwave, covered, on High for 1½ minutes. Stir and continue to microwave, covered on High for 1½ minutes.

3 Stir in the cilantro and lime juice and top with tortilla strips.

MAKE IT TO GO

Combine ingredients in the mug as directed in Step 1. Cover mug, close vent and pack with ice packs. Pack lime juice in a small sealed travel-safe container with ice packs. Pack cilantro and tortilla strips in separate containers or ziplock bags. When ready to eat, open vent and continue as directed in Step 2.

tip

Use leftover pulled pork or ham in place of the cooked chicken.

WHITE CHICKEN CHILI

Warm, filling and super easy to prepare, this white chicken chili is the ideal lunch on a cold winter day. It is super easy to prepare if you begin with leftover cooked chicken or a rotisserie chicken.

MAKES 1 SERVING | 1 (20 oz/625 g) microwave mug with vented cover

$\frac{1}{2}$ cup (125 mL) chopped cooked chicken

$\frac{1}{2}$ cup (125 mL) canned Great Northern beans, drained and rinsed

$\frac{1}{4}$ cup (60 mL) frozen corn

$\frac{1}{4}$ cup (60 mL) ready-to-use chicken broth

3 tbsp (45 mL) salsa verde

1 tsp (5 mL) dry minced onion

$\frac{1}{2}$ tsp (2 mL) ground cumin

Salt and ground black pepper

Tortilla chips, shredded Monterey Jack cheese and minced cilantro (optional)

tip

White chicken chili, due to its color, typically begins with Great Northern beans, which are large white beans and are readily available canned. Cannellini beans or navy beans could be substituted for the Great Northern beans.

1 In the mug, stir together chicken, beans, corn, broth, salsa verde, onion and cumin. Season to taste with salt and pepper.

2 Microwave, covered, on High for $2\frac{1}{2}$ to 3 minutes. Let stand, covered, for 1 minute. Top with chips, cheese and cilantro (if using.)

MAKE IT TO GO

Combine ingredients in the mug as as directed in Step 1. Cover mug, close vent and pack with ice packs. Pack tortilla chips, cheese and minced cilantro (if using) in separate containers or ziplock bags. When ready to eat, open vent and continue as directed in Step 2.

TWO-BEAN TURKEY CHILI

This healthy alternative to beef chili is packed with flavor in every bite. You can substitute your favorite beans for the kidney beans and black beans.

MAKES 1 SERVING | 1 (20 oz/625 g) microwave mug with vented cover

1 cup (250 mL) canned diced tomatoes with juice

½ cup (125 mL) crumbled cooked ground turkey

¼ cup (60 mL) canned kidney beans, drained and rinsed

¼ cup (60 mL) canned black beans, drained and rinsed

1 tbsp (15 mL) finely chopped green pepper

2 tsp (10 mL) dry minced onion

1 tsp (5 mL) chili powder

½ tsp (2 mL) ground cumin

¼ tsp (1 mL) salt

1 In the mug, combine tomatoes, turkey, kidney beans, black beans, green pepper, onion, chili powder, cumin and salt. Stir well.

2 Microwave, covered, on High for 2 to 2½ minutes. Stir well.

MAKE IT TO GO

Combine ingredients in the mug as directed in Step 1. Cover mug, close vent and pack with ice packs. When ready to eat, open vent and continue as directed in Step 2.

GAME DAY CHILI

Who doesn't love a piping hot bowl of chili while watching the big game? This chili will make any day a winner.

½ cup (125 mL) crumbled cooked ground beef

⅓ cup (75 mL) canned diced tomatoes, with juice

¼ cup (60 mL) canned kidney beans, drained and rinsed

2 tbsp (30 mL) finely chopped onion

½ tsp (2 mL) dry minced garlic

½ tsp (2 mL) ground cumin

½ tsp (2 mL) chili powder

⅛ tsp (0.5 mL) hot pepper flakes

1 In the mug, combine beef, tomatoes, beans, onion, garlic, cumin, chili powder and pepper flakes. Stir well.

2 Microwave, covered, on High for $2\frac{1}{2}$ to 3 minutes.

MAKE IT TO GO

Combine ingredients in the mug as directed in Step 1. Cover mug, close vent and pack with ice packs. When ready to eat, open vent and continue as directed in Step 2.

tips

Brown the ground beef the night before and refrigerate it overnight. In the morning you can quickly combine the chilled beef with the remaining ingredients.

You can substitute your favorite cooked beans for the kidney beans.

BLACK BEAN AND FARRO CHILI

If you are not familiar with farro, you are in for a treat. The ancient grain is actually a form of wheat, and the kernels resemble orzo or brown rice with a delightful chewy, nutty flavor. Cook the farro in boiling, salted water according to the package directions. Use what you need for this chili and, if any extra remains, cover and refrigerate. Toss the cooked farro with a vinaigrette for a quick, delicious salad or use in place of cooked brown rice in a casserole.

MAKES 1 SERVING | 1 (20 oz/625 g) microwave mug with vented cover

⅔ cup (150 mL) canned black beans, drained and rinsed

½ cup (125 mL) cooked farro

3 tbsp (45 mL) salsa or pico de gallo

1½ tsp (7 mL) chili powder

1 tsp (5 mL) dry minced onion

¼ tsp (1 mL) garlic powder

Salt and ground black pepper

½ cup (125 mL) tomato juice

1 In the mug, combine beans, farro, salsa, chili powder, onion and garlic powder. Season to taste with salt and pepper. Stir in the tomato juice.

2 Microwave, covered, on High for 2 to 2½ minutes. Let rest 1 minute.

MAKE IT TO GO

Combine ingredients in the mug as directed in Step 1. Cover the mug, close vent and pack with ice packs. When ready to eat, open vent and continue as directed in Step 2.

VEGETARIAN CHILI

Vegetarian chili never tasted so good. You won't miss the meat in this delicious, thick and easy-to-prepare chili.

MAKES 1 SERVING | 1 (20 oz/625 g) microwave mug with vented cover

½ cup (125 mL) canned kidney beans, drained and rinsed

¼ cup (60 mL) canned chickpeas, drained and rinsed

¼ cup (60 mL) frozen corn

2 tbsp (30 mL) finely chopped red bell pepper

1½ tsp (7 mL) chili powder

1 tsp (5 mL) dry minced onion

¼ tsp (60 mL) ground cumin

Salt and ground black pepper

¾ cup (175 mL) crushed tomatoes

1 In the mug, combine beans, chickpeas, corn, red pepper, chili powder, onion and cumin. Season to taste with salt and pepper. Stir in the tomatoes.

2 Microwave, covered, on High for 3 minutes.

MAKE IT TO GO

Combine ingredients in the mug as directed in Step 1. Cover mug, close vent and pack with ice packs. When ready to eat, open vent and continue as directed in Step 2.

tips

Substitute your favorite beans, such as pinto beans or Great northern beans, for the kidney beans and chickpeas.

Chickpeas are also called garbanzo beans. Look for cans of these beans with the other canned beans or shelved with Hispanic and Latino foods.

pastas

PASTA PRIMAVERA

Anytime you hear the name pasta primavera, it means that a delicious pasta and vegetable dish is on the menu. This tasty and healthy version features broccoli, peas and carrots with a Parmesan herb flavor.

MAKES 1 SERVING | 1 (20 oz/625 g) microwave mug with vented cover

½ cup (125 mL) frozen chopped broccoli

2 tbsp (30 mL) frozen peas

2 tbsp (30 mL) finely chopped carrots

2 tbsp (30 mL) ready-to-use vegetable or chicken broth or water

1 tbsp (15 mL) butter, cut into small cubes

½ tsp (2 mL) dried Italian seasoning

⅛ tsp (0.5 mL) garlic powder

Salt and ground black pepper

1 cup (250 mL) cooked penne or ziti pasta

2 tbsp (30 mL) grated Parmesan cheese

1 In the mug, combine broccoli, peas, carrots, broth, butter, Italian seasoning and garlic powder. Season to taste with salt and pepper.

2 Microwave, covered, on High for 2½ to 3 minutes. Stir in the penne and Parmesan cheese. Continue to microwave, covered, on High for 30 seconds to 1 minute.

MAKE IT TO GO

Combine ingredients in the mug as directed in Step 1. Cover mug, close vent and pack with ice packs. Pack the pasta and Parmesan together in a separate container or ziplock bag with ice packs. When ready to eat, open vent and continue as directed in Step 2. If vegetables are thawed, reduce the cooking time to 2 minutes.

tip

Two ounces (60 g) of penne, cooked in boiling, salted water according to the package directions, will make about 1 cup (250 mL) cooked pasta. If desired, substitute other pasta shapes, such as farfalle or rotini, for the penne.

HAMMY MAC AND CHEESE

Comfort in a mug describes this recipe. You can now prepare macaroni and cheese that brings back all the best memories of your childhood. Begin with precooked macaroni or follow the steps in the variation to cook the macaroni. Use whichever method you prefer.

MAKES 1 SERVING | 1 (20 oz/625 g) microwave mug with vented cover

1¼ cups (310 mL) cooked macaroni

½ cup (125 mL) shredded Cheddar cheese

¼ cup (60 mL) finely diced fully cooked ham

¼ cup (60 mL) milk

¼ tsp (1 mL) salt

1 In the mug, combine macaroni, cheese, ham, milk and salt. Stir well.

2 Microwave, covered, on High for 1½ to 2 minutes. Stir and continue to microwave, uncovered, on High for 1 minute.

tip

Of course, you may prefer traditional macaroni and cheese, and if that is the case, omit the ham cubes and proceed as directed.

MAKE IT TO GO

Combine ingredients in the mug as directed in Step 1. Cover mug, close vent and pack with ice packs. When ready to eat, open vent and continue as directed in Step 2.

variation

Starting with uncooked macaroni? It just takes an extra couple of steps.

In the mug, combine ½ cup (125 mL) uncooked elbow macaroni, ½ cup (125 mL) water and ¼ tsp (1 mL) salt. Stir well. Place a paper towel in the microwave oven to absorb moisture, then place mug on the paper towel. Microwave, covered, on High for 3 minutes. Stir and continue to microwave, covered, on High, for 2 minutes. Stir and continue to microwave, covered, on High, for 1½ minutes. Stir in milk, cheese and ham. Microwave, uncovered, on High for 1 minute. Let stand, covered, for 1 minute.

CHILI MAC

When Roxanne's daughter was in elementary school, the only way she would eat chili was if a large amount of elbow macaroni was stirred in. It worked, because as an adult she loves chili, macaroni added or not. If you are on the fence as to whether you like chili or not, try this recipe. The macaroni addition is tasty and you can always top it with shredded Cheddar cheese.

MAKES 1 SERVING | 1 (20 oz/625 g) microwave mug with vented cover

½ cup (125 mL) canned diced tomatoes with onions and garlic, with juice

1 tbsp (15 mL) finely chopped onion

1 tbsp (15 mL) grated carrots

1 tsp (5 mL) chili powder

½ tsp (2 mL) ground cumin

½ tsp (2 mL) Worcestershire sauce

¼ tsp (1 mL) salt

½ cup (125 mL) cooked elbow macaroni

1 In the mug, combine tomatoes, onion, carrots, chili powder, cumin, Worcestershire sauce and salt. Stir well. Gently stir in the cooked macaroni.

2 Microwave, covered, on High for 2 minutes. Stir and continue to microwave, covered, on High for 1½ minutes.

MAKE IT TO GO

Combine ingredients in the mug as directed in Step 1. Cover mug, close vent and pack with ice packs. When ready to eat, open vent and continue as directed in Step 2.

tips

Substitute any small to medium cooked pasta for the cooked elbow macaroni.

For quick and easy preparation of this recipe on a busy morning, plan ahead so you have cooked pasta ready to use at a moment's notice. When preparing a pasta dish, cook a little extra, place in a ziplock bag and freeze or refrigerate for use within three days.

CHEESY RAVIOLI

Oh, so simple! This ravioli captures lots of cheesy goodness and is ready in just minutes.

MAKES 1 SERVING | 1 (20 oz/625 g) microwave mug with vented cover

8 frozen ravioli, preferably cheese-filled

¼ cup (60 mL) spaghetti sauce or marinara sauce

¼ cup (60 mL) water

⅓ cup (75 mL) shredded Italian blend cheese or mozzarella cheese

1 In the mug, combine ravioli, spaghetti sauce and water. Stir to coat ravioli with sauce.

2 Place a paper towel in the microwave oven to absorb moisture. Microwave, covered, for 3 minutes. Stir and continue to microwave, covered, for 3 minutes.

3 Sprinkle with cheese. Cover and let rest for 1 minute.

MAKE IT TO GO

Combine ingredients in the mug as directed in Step 1. Cover mug, close vent and pack with ice packs. Pack cheese in a ziplock bag with ice packs. When ready to eat, continue as directed in Step 2.

SPAGHETTI AND MEATBALLS

Roxanne's daughter would definitely rank spaghetti and meatballs as one of her all-time favorites. Roxanne prepares and cooks the meatballs ahead and freezes them for quick and easy use. She also makes her favorite marinara sauce and freezes the sauce in ½-cup (125 mL) portions. Now her daughter can enjoy her favorite meal whenever she desires.

MAKES 1 SERVING | 1 (20 oz/625 g) microwave mug with vented cover

3 frozen fully-cooked meatballs, preferably Italian style

½ cup (125 mL) marinara sauce

1 cup (250 mL) cooked spaghetti or angel hair pasta

1 tbsp (15 mL) grated Parmesan cheese

1 In the mug, combine meatballs and marinara sauce.

2 Microwave, covered, on High for 3 minutes. Stir in spaghetti. Continue to microwave, uncovered, for 1 to 1½ minutes or until heated through. Sprinkle with Parmesan cheese.

tips

Packages of precooked pasta shapes are available and make this recipe even quicker to prepare. Substitute a precooked packaged pasta such as penne for the spaghetti and proceed as directed.

For a fresh flavor, stir in 1½ tbsp (22 mL) chopped fresh basil with the marinara sauce.

MAKE IT TO GO

Combine ingredients in the mug as directed in Step 1. Cover mug, close vent and pack with ice packs. Pack cooked pasta and Parmesan in separate containers or ziplock bags with ice packs. When ready to eat, open vent and continue as directed in Step 2.

SPAGHETTI PIZZA PIE

This recipe combines the best of spaghetti and pizza. Make it whenever you have leftover cooked spaghetti. Trust us, the flavor will be fresh, delicious and guaranteed not to taste like leftovers.

MAKES 1 SERVING | 1 (20 oz/625 g) microwave mug with vented cover

1 large egg

1 tbsp (15 mL) grated Parmesan cheese

Salt and ground black pepper

1 cup (250 mL) cooked spaghetti

⅓ cup (75 mL) marinara sauce or pizza sauce

⅓ cup (75 mL) shredded Italian blend cheese or mozzarella cheese

6 slices turkey pepperoni, thinly sliced

---

tip

Substitute your favorite prepared or leftover spaghetti sauce for the marinara or pizza sauce.

1 In the mug, whisk together the egg and Parmesan cheese. Season with salt and pepper as desired. Add spaghetti, stirring until it is evenly coated with the egg. Spoon sauce over the spaghetti. Top with the Italian cheese and pepperoni.

2 Microwave, covered, on High for 2 minutes. Let rest 1 minute.

MAKE IT TO GO

Combine ingredients in the mug as directed in Step 1. Cover mug, close vent and pack with ice packs. When ready to eat, open vent and continue as directed in Step 2.

CHEESEBURGER PASTA

When you want the flavors of a cheeseburger, this quick and easy-to-serve mug meal is what you need.

MAKES 1 SERVING | 1 (20 oz/625 g) microwave mug with vented cover

1¼ cups (310 mL) cooked farfalle (bow-tie) or rotini pasta

½ cup (125 mL) crumbled cooked ground beef

¼ cup (60 mL) milk

1 tbsp (15 mL) ketchup

1 tsp (5 mL) prepared mustard

Salt and ground black pepper

⅔ cup (150 mL) shredded Cheddar cheese

tip

Substitute cooked elbow macaroni for the farfalle, if desired.

1 In the mug, combine pasta and ground beef. In a small bowl, stir together milk, ketchup and mustard. Season to taste with salt and pepper. Pour milk mixture over pasta. Stir in cheese.

2 Microwave, covered, on High for 1½ minutes. Stir and continue to microwave, covered, on High for 1 minute. Let rest for 1 minute.

MAKE IT TO GO

Combine ingredients in the mug as directed in Step 1. Cover mug, close vent and pack with ice packs. When ready to eat, open vent and continue as directed in Step 2.

CHEESY ROTINI WITH HAM AND PEAS

The cream cheese in this mug meal reminds us of a ham version of beef stroganoff. It is packed with cheesy goodness and studded with tasty green peas. It has such a wonderful flavor that you will resist the temptation to go out to buy a fast-food burger in a bag.

MAKES 1 SERVING | 1 (20 oz/625 g) microwave mug with vented cover

2 tbsp (30 mL) butter, cut into small cubes

2 tbsp (30 mL) finely chopped onion

1½ tbsp (22 mL) all-purpose flour

⅓ cup + 2 tbsp (105 mL) milk

1 oz (30 g) cream cheese, softened

¾ cup (175 mL) cooked rotini

½ cup (125 mL) fully cooked ham cubes

⅓ cup (75 mL) frozen peas

2 tbsp (30 mL) sour cream

¼ tsp (1 mL) garlic powder

1 tbsp (15 mL) chopped chives (optional)

tip

Use any medium-size cooked pasta in place of the rotini. We used multicolor rotini for a change.

1 In the mug, combine butter and onion.

2 Microwave, covered, on High for 1½ minutes. Stir in flour. Add milk and cream cheese. Microwave, covered, on High for 1 minute.

3 Stir in rotini, ham, peas, sour cream and garlic powder and continue to microwave, covered, on High for 45 seconds to 1 minute. Sprinkle with chives, if using.

MAKE IT TO GO

Combine ingredients in the mug as directed in Step 1. Cover mug, close vent and pack with ice packs. Pack flour in a separate ziplock bag. Pack milk and cream cheese in a sealed travel-safe container with ice packs. Pack pasta, ham, peas, sour cream and garlic powder in a sealed container with ice packs. Pack chives in ziplock bag. When ready to eat, continue as directed in Step 2.

CREAMY TORTELLINI WITH TOMATOES AND SPINACH

This is the pasta dish to make when you crave something delicious, yet a little different from the typical red-sauce pasta.

MAKES 1 SERVING | 1 (20 oz/625 g) microwave mug with vented cover

¾ cup (175 mL) refrigerated cheese-filled tortellini (about 18 tortellini)

⅛ tsp (0.5 mL) garlic powder

Salt and ground black pepper

⅓ cup (75 mL) ready-to-use chicken broth

⅓ cup (75 mL) coarsely chopped fresh spinach

¼ cup (60 mL) canned diced tomatoes with juice

1 tbsp (15 mL) cream cheese, softened

1 tbsp (15 mL) grated Parmesan cheese

¼ tsp (1 mL) dried Italian seasoning

1 In the mug, combine tortellini and garlic powder. Season to taste with salt and pepper. Add broth and stir to coat tortellini with broth.

2 Place a paper towel in the microwave oven to absorb moisture. Microwave, covered, on High for 3 minutes.

3 Stir in spinach, tomatoes, cream cheese, Parmesan cheese and Italian seasoning. Continue to microwave, covered, on High for 1 minute. Let rest 1 minute.

tip

Substitute 3 tbsp (45 mL) frozen chopped spinach, thawed and drained, for the fresh spinach leaves.

MAKE IT TO GO

Combine ingredients in the mug as directed in Step 1. Cover mug, close vent and pack with ice packs. Pack spinach, tomatoes, cream cheese, Parmesan cheese and Italian seasoning in a separate container with ice packs. When ready to eat, open vent and continue as directed in Step 2.

PENNE PESTO CHICKEN

A healthy lunch or dinner in less than 5 minutes! Now you can enjoy a delicious meal no matter how busy your day.

MAKES 1 SERVING | 1 (20 oz/625 g) microwave mug with vented cover

1 cup (250 mL) cooked penne

½ cup (125 mL) chopped cooked chicken

2 tbsp (30 mL) pesto sauce

⅓ cup (75 mL) sliced cherry or grape tomatoes

1 tbsp (15 mL) grated Parmesan cheese

1 In the mug, combine penne, chicken and pesto.

2 Microwave, covered, on High for 1 minute.

3 Stir in tomatoes. Continue to microwave, covered, on High for 1½ minutes. Sprinkle with Parmesan cheese. Let stand for 1 minute.

tips

Substitute 1 cup (250 mL) of any type of cooked pasta for the penne.

Make a vegetarian meal by omitting the chicken and increasing the tomatoes to ½ cup (125 mL).

MAKE IT TO GO

Combine ingredients in the mug as directed in Step 1. Cover mug, close vent and pack with ice packs. Pack tomatoes and Parmesan in separate containers or ziplock bags with ice packs. When ready to eat, open vent and continue as directed in Step 2.

BROWN RICE NOODLES WITH VEGETABLES

Brown rice noodles are easy to prepare. Just stir the noodles into boiling water and let stand for about 5 minutes.

MAKES 1 SERVING | 1 (20 oz/625 g) microwave mug with vented cover

1⅔ cups (400 mL) water, divided

1 packet (2 oz/60 g) brown rice noodles

1 tsp (5 mL) sesame oil

¾ cup (175 mL) chopped fresh vegetables (see tip)

2 tbsp (30 mL) finely chopped red bell pepper

1½ tbsp (22 mL) soy sauce

¼ tsp (1 mL) ground ginger

¼ tsp (1 mL) garlic powder

½ tsp (2 mL) sesame seeds

1 In the mug, pour 1½ cups (375 mL) water. Microwave on High 3 to 4 minutes or until water begins to boil. Break the noodles apart and stir into the hot water. Let stand 5 minutes. Drain. In a small bowl, stir together the noodles and sesame oil. Set aside.

2 In the mug, combine vegetables, red pepper, soy sauce, ginger and garlic. Stir in remaining 2 tbsp (30 mL) water.

3 Microwave, covered, on High for 2 to 2½ minutes or until the vegetables are crisp-tender. Stir in the noodles and sesame seeds.

tip

Use your favorite vegetables in this recipe. Some favorites include very small broccoli florets, shredded carrots or trimmed and halved pea pods; these can be combined with chopped celery or chopped onion. If fresh are not available, substitute frozen stir-fry vegetable blends.

MAKE IT TO GO

Prepare as directed in Step 1. Toss noodles with sesame oil and pack in separate container or ziplock bag. Combine ingredients in mug as directed in Step 2. Cover mug, close vent and pack with ice packs. When ready to eat, open vent and continue as directed in Step 3, increasing time if noodles are cold.

MUG PAD THAI

Pad Thai is a stir-fry dish that features rice noodles flavored by a delicious sauce. Capture some of those flavors in this mug recipe inspired by the classic Thai dish. This version calls for cooked chicken, but feel free to omit the chicken and increase the bean sprouts to ½ cup (125 mL).

MAKES 1 SERVING | 1 (20 oz/625 g) microwave mug with vented cover

1 cup (250 mL) cooked rice noodles

¼ cup (60 mL) chopped cooked chicken

¼ cup (60 mL) fresh bean sprouts

3 tbsp (45 mL) pad thai sauce (see tip)

3 tbsp (45 mL) water

⅛ tsp (0.5 mL) garlic powder

2 tbsp (30 mL) lightly salted roasted peanuts, chopped

1 tsp (5 mL) chopped fresh cilantro (optional)

1 In the mug, combine noodles, chicken and bean sprouts. In a small bowl, stir together pad thai sauce, water and garlic powder. Stir sauce mixture into noodles.

2 Microwave, uncovered, on High for 2 minutes.

3 Just before serving, sprinkle with peanuts and cilantro (if using).

tips

Rice noodles are now available precooked in individual serving packets. Look for them shelved with Asian foods at your grocery store. If you prefer to prepare your own rice noodles, cook according to package directions.

Bottled pad thai sauce is shelved with the Asian foods.

MAKE IT TO GO

Combine ingredients in the mug as directed in Step 1. Cover mug, close vent and pack with ice packs. Pack peanuts in a ziplock bag. Pack cilantro (if using) in a separate ziplock bag with ice packs. When ready to eat, open vent and continue as directed in Step 2.

RAMEN MUG

Restaurants that specialize in ramen make a deeply flavored broth, filled with distinctive, chewy noodles and garnished with an array of toppings. This recipe begins with instant noodles, but we have added lots of flavor.

MAKES 1 SERVING | 1 (20 oz/625 g) microwave mug with vented cover

⅓ cup (125 mL) chopped cooked chicken or pork

2 tbsp (30 mL) shredded carrots

2 tbsp (30 mL) frozen chopped spinach

¼ tsp (1 mL) ground ginger

⅛ tsp (0.5 mL) garlic powder

Dash hot pepper flakes, or to taste

1⅓ cups (325 mL) ready-to-use chicken broth

½ package (3 oz/90 g) ramen noodle soup

Halved soft-cooked egg (see tip), sliced green onion, or sliced radish (optional)

1 In the mug, stir together chicken, carrots, spinach, ginger, garlic powder and pepper flakes. Pour in broth.

2 Place a paper towel in the microwave oven to absorb moisture. Microwave, uncovered, on High for 3 minutes or until broth is just beginning to boil. Set ramen seasoning mix aside for another use or discard. Break noodles apart and stir into broth. Microwave, uncovered, on High for 1½ to 2 minutes, or until noodles are tender. Cover and let rest 2 minutes.

3 Just before serving, top with egg, green onion or radish (if using) as desired.

tip

The egg often served on top of a bowl of ramen is a soft, hard-cooked egg, or sometimes called a medium hard-cooked egg. It means that the egg is cooked until the white is firm and the yolk is still a little moist or jammy. When ready to serve the ramen, peel the egg and slice in half.

MAKE IT TO GO

Combine ingredients in the mug as directed in Step 1. Cover mug, close vent and pack with ice packs. Pack ramen noodles in a ziplock bag. Pack toppings (if using) in separate containers or ziplock bags with ice packs. When ready to eat, open vent and continue as directed in Step 2.

vegetables and grains

MEXICAN-STYLE STREET CORN

Corn has always been a pillar of Mexican cuisine, and recently street corn has become a popular *antojito* (little craving or street food) found all over Mexico and the United States. The tang of the lime juice and cheese complements the corn and produces a flavor that is unique yet not overpowering.

MAKES 1 SERVING | 1 (20 oz/ 625 g) microwave mug with vented cover

1¼ cups (310 mL) frozen yellow corn, thawed

1 tbsp (15 mL) butter, cut into small cubes

1 tbsp (15 mL) light or regular mayonnaise

1 tbsp (15 mL) freshly squeezed lime juice

Salt and ground black pepper

2 tbsp (30 mL) crumbled Cotija cheese, crumbled feta or grated Parmesan cheese

1 tbsp (15 mL) chopped fresh cilantro

1 In the mug, combine corn, butter, mayonnaise and lime juice. Season to taste with salt and pepper.

2 Microwave, covered, on High for 1½ minutes. Stir and continue to microwave, uncovered, on High for 1½ minutes. Sprinkle with cheese and cilantro.

MAKE IT TO GO

Combine ingredients in the mug as directed in Step 1. Cover mug, close vent and pack with ice packs. Pack cheese and cilantro in separate containers or ziplock bags with ice packs. When ready to eat, open vent and continue as directed in Step 2.

tip

In season, substitute fresh corn cut from the cob for the frozen corn.

RED BEANS AND RICE

Red beans and rice is a Creole dish from Louisiana. History tells us that traditionally this was prepared with leftover meat and vegetables and simmered all day on Monday, then served over hot rice. No need to take it slow when this can be just as tasty out of the microwave.

MAKES 1 SERVING | 1 (20 oz/625 g) microwave mug with vented cover

2 tbsp (30 mL) finely chopped onion

2 tbsp (30 mL) finely chopped celery

2 tbsp (30 mL) finely chopped green bell pepper

1 tsp (5 mL) olive oil

$\frac{3}{4}$ cup (175 mL) canned red beans, drained and rinsed

$\frac{1}{2}$ cup (125 mL) diced smoked sausage or diced fully cooked ham

$\frac{1}{3}$ cup (75 mL) tomato sauce

$\frac{1}{4}$ tsp (1 mL) hot pepper sauce

$\frac{1}{8}$ tsp (0.5 mL) dried thyme leaves

$\frac{1}{3}$ cup (75 mL) cooked white rice

1 tbsp (15 mL) chopped green onion

tip

Substitute kidney beans or pinto beans for red beans.

1 In the mug, combine onion, celery, green pepper and oil.

2 Microwave, covered, on High for $1\frac{1}{2}$ minutes.

3 Stir in beans, sausage, tomato sauce, hot pepper sauce and thyme. Microwave, covered, on High for $1\frac{1}{2}$ to 2 minutes. Stir in rice and sprinkle with green onion. (Traditionally rice is placed on top of the bean mixture, but for easy mug enjoyment, we find it best to stir the rice in, then sprinkle with green onions.)

MAKE IT TO GO

Combine ingredients in the mug as directed in Step 1. Cover mug, close vent and pack with ice packs. Pack beans, sausage, tomato sauce, hot pepper sauce and thyme in a separate container with ice packs. Pack rice and green onions in separate containers with ice packs. When ready to eat, open vent and continue as directed in Step 2.

FRIED RICE

Fried rice is the perfect recipe to use up leftover rice. You can also use leftover cooked vegetables in place of the frozen vegetables. Pass the soy sauce and enjoy a flavor-filled meal.

MAKES 1 SERVING | 1 (20 oz/625 g) microwave mug with vented cover

1 cup (250 mL) cooked white rice

¼ cup (60 mL) frozen mixed vegetables

1 green onion, chopped

1 clove garlic, minced

1½ tbsp (22 mL) soy sauce

1 tsp (5 mL) rice vinegar

½ tsp (2 mL) sesame oil

1 large egg, beaten

tip

Add an extra splash of soy sauce, if desired, when serving.

1 In the mug, combine rice, vegetables, green onion, garlic, soy sauce, rice vinegar and sesame oil.

2 Microwave, covered, on High for 1½ minutes.

3 Pour egg on top of rice mixture. Continue to microwave, covered, on High for 1½ minutes. Stir thoroughly.

MAKE IT TO GO

Combine ingredients in the mug as directed in Step 1. Cover mug, close vent and pack with ice packs. Crack egg into a separate container and pack with ice packs. When ready to eat, open vent and continue as directed in Step 2.

SALSA RICE BOWL

Rice bowl or burrito bowl, call it what you like, we call it delicious, satisfying and much easier than standing in line and ordering your custom bowl ingredients from the local eatery.

MAKES 1 SERVING | 1 (20 oz/625 g) microwave mug with vented cover

1 tsp (5 mL) olive oil

2 tbsp (30 mL) finely chopped onion

3 tbsp (45 mL) finely chopped bell pepper

1 cup (250 mL) packaged 90-second Spanish rice

½ cup (125 mL) crumbled cooked ground beef or chopped cooked chicken

¼ cup (60 mL) canned red or black beans, drained and rinsed

⅓ cup (75 mL) salsa or taco sauce

2 tbsp (30 mL) shredded Cheddar cheese

Chopped fresh cilantro, chopped grape tomatoes, pickled jalapeño slices, sliced radishes or chopped green onions (optional)

1 In the mug, combine oil, onion and pepper.

2 Microwave, uncovered, on High for 1½ minutes. Scoop Spanish rice into mug and stir, breaking it up with a spoon. Stir in ground beef, beans and salsa. Continue to microwave, uncovered, on High for 2 minutes, stirring once halfway through.

3 Sprinkle with shredded cheese. Garnish with optional ingredients, if using.

MAKE IT TO GO

Combine ingredients in the mug as directed in Step 1. Cover mug, close vent and pack with ice packs. Pack Spanish rice in a separate container with ice packs. Pack ground beef, beans and salsa in a separate container with ice packs. Place Cheddar cheese and optional ingredients (if using) in separate containers or ziplock bags with ice packs.

tips

Place remaining 90-second Spanish rice in a container and refrigerate to serve another time or in another recipe.

Substitute 1 cup (250 mL) cooked rice and ½ tsp (2 mL) chili powder for the 90-second Spanish rice.

RISOTTO WITH MUSHROOMS AND SPINACH

There are certain days when nothing is quite as satisfying as a bowl of warm risotto with vegetables and cheese. No need to make a full recipe in a saucepan on the stove when a mug meal will answer the craving.

MAKES 1 SERVING | 1 (20 oz/625 g) microwave mug with vented cover

1 tbsp (15 mL) butter, cut into small pieces

1 cup (250 mL) ready-to-use chicken broth

¼ cup (60 mL) Arborio rice

¼ tsp (1 mL) granulated garlic

¼ tsp (1 mL) salt

½ cup (125 mL) coarsely chopped mushrooms

½ cup (125 mL) coarsely chopped fresh spinach

2 tbsp (30 mL) grated Parmesan cheese

1 In the mug, combine butter, broth, rice, garlic and salt.

2 Place a double layer of paper towels on the microwave floor. Microwave, covered, on Medium (50%) power for 7 minutes.

3 Stir in the mushrooms and spinach. Microwave, covered, on Medium (50%) power for 2 minutes. Let stand, covered, for 5 minutes. Stir in cheese. Serve warm.

tip

Omit spinach and substitute fresh asparagus cut into 1½ inch (4 cm) pieces.

MAKE IT TO GO

In the mug, combine ingredients as directed in Step 1. Cover mug, close vent and pack with ice packs. Pack mushrooms, spinach and cheese in separate containers or ziplock bags with ice packs. When ready to eat, open vent and continue as directed in Step 2.

CHICKPEA MUG WITH COUSCOUS

Couscous is the ultimate quick-cooking, healthy convenience food. This semolina or wheat pasta is precooked and dried so it can be prepared very quickly. Here, the couscous is combined with chickpeas, artichokes, roasted red peppers and feta cheese for a classic Mediterranean flavor.

MAKES 1 SERVING | 1 (20 oz/625 g) microwave mug with vented cover

½ cup (125 mL) canned chickpeas, drained and rinsed

¼ cup (60 mL) chopped, canned artichoke hearts, drained

¼ cup (60 mL) chopped roasted red pepper, drained

½ tsp (2 mL) olive oil

½ tsp (2 mL) dried Italian seasoning

Salt and ground black pepper

⅔ cup (150 mL) ready-to-use vegetable or chicken broth

⅓ cup (75 mL) uncooked couscous (see tip)

Feta cheese crumbles (optional)

1 In the mug, combine chickpeas, artichoke hearts, red pepper, oil and Italian seasoning. Season to taste with salt and pepper. Stir in broth.

2 Microwave, covered, on High for 2 minutes or until liquid is steaming and almost boiling. Stir in couscous. Cover and let stand for 5 minutes. Sprinkle with feta cheese (if using).

MAKE IT TO GO

Combine ingredients in the mug as directed in Step 1. Cover mug, close vent and pack with ice packs. Pack couscous and feta cheese (if using) in separate containers or ziplock bags with ice packs. When ready to eat, open vent and continue as directed in Step 2.

tip

Regular couscous reconstitutes in about 5 minutes when stirred into boiling liquid. Israeli or pearl couscous is a toasted pasta shaped into tiny balls. While both are delicious, do not use Israeli couscous in this recipe as it requires much longer cooking time.

MEDITERRANEAN-INSPIRED QUINOA, TOMATO AND FETA

Protein-rich quinoa makes this delicious vegetarian dish a nutritious, complete meal.

MAKES 1 SERVING | 1 (20 oz/625 g) microwave mug with vented cover

1 cup (250 mL) cooked quinoa

⅔ cup (150 mL) canned diced tomatoes with basil, garlic and oregano, with juice

2 tbsp (30 mL) finely chopped red onion

2 tbsp (30 mL) sliced, pitted kalamata or black olives

¼ tsp (1 mL) dried Italian seasoning

Salt and ground black pepper

3 tbsp (45 mL) feta cheese crumbles

Minced fresh flat-leaf (Italian) parsley (optional)

1 In the mug, combine quinoa, tomatoes, red onion, olives and Italian seasoning. Season to taste with salt and pepper.

2 Microwave, covered, on High for 1½ to 2 minutes. Sprinkle with feta and parsley (if using).

MAKE IT TO GO

Combine ingredients in the mug as directed in Step 1. Cover mug, close vent and pack with ice packs. Pack feta and parsley (if using) in separate containers or ziplock bags with ice packs. When ready to eat, open vent and continue as directed in Step 2.

TORTILLA CHIPS WITH EGGS, SALSA AND CHEESE

Chilaquiles are popular on many menus. Crisp tortilla chips are cooked with scrambled eggs, salsa and cheese to create a stick-to-your-ribs breakfast or lunch. Give this recipe a try and see what all the buzz is about.

MAKES 1 SERVING | 1 (20 oz/625 g) microwave mug with vented cover

Nonstick cooking spray

$1/2$ cup + 2 tbsp (155 mL) crushed tortilla chips, divided

2 large eggs

$1/4$ cup (60 mL) salsa

5 tbsp (75 mL) shredded Cheddar cheese, divided

Salt and ground black pepper

1 tbsp (15 mL) sour cream

1 tbsp (15 mL) chopped fresh cilantro

3 slices pickled jalapeños, drained

1 Spray the mug with nonstick spray. Place $1/2$ cup (125 mL) crushed tortilla chips in mug.

2 In a small bowl, whisk together eggs, salsa, and 3 tbsp (45 mL) shredded cheese. Season to taste with salt and pepper. Microwave, uncovered, on High for 3 minutes.

3 Top with remaining 2 tbsp (30 mL) crushed tortilla chips, remaining 2 tbsp (30 mL) cheese, sour cream, cilantro and pickled jalapeños.

MAKE IT TO GO

Prepare the recipe as directed through Step 1. Cover mug, close vent and pack. Combine eggs, salsa, 3 tbsp (45 mL) cheese, salt and pepper in a sealed, travel-safe container and pack with ice packs. Pack sour cream and remaining 2 tbsp (30 mL) cheese in a small, sealed travel-safe container with ice packs. Place cilantro and jalapeños in a ziplock bag with ice packs. When ready to eat, proceed as directed in Step 2.

beef, pork, chicken and turkey

SLOPPY JOES

Sloppy Joes are always great served on a bun. For a fun school lunch, leave the bun at home and send a bag of scoop-size corn chips to dip in the seasoned meat. Add celery and carrot sticks and a fruit-flavored yogurt to complete the lunch-box meal.

MAKES 1 SERVING | 1 (20 oz/625 g) microwave mug with vented cover

1 cup (250 mL) crumbled cooked ground beef or ground turkey

1/3 cup (75 mL) tomato sauce

1 tbsp (15 mL) packed dark brown sugar

2 tsp (10 mL) dry minced onion

1 tsp (5 mL) Worcestershire sauce

1/4 tsp (1 mL) salt

1 hamburger bun, split

1 In the mug, combine beef, tomato sauce, brown sugar, onion, Worcestershire sauce and salt. Stir to combine.

2 Microwave, covered, on High for 2 minutes. Spoon onto hamburger bun.

MAKE IT TO GO

Combine ingredients in the mug as directed in Step 1. Cover mug, close vent and pack with ice packs. Pack hamburger bun in a ziplock bag. When ready to eat, open vent and continue as directed in Step 2.

BEEFY SALSA POTATOES

This is a full meal that satisfies like no other. Chunks of potatoes, ground beef, salsa and cheese will remind you of a southwestern stuffed baked potato. Add a dollop of sour cream to complete the sensation.

MAKES 1 SERVING | 1 (20 oz/625 g) microwave mug with vented cover

½ cup (125 mL) refrigerated diced potatoes with onions

½ cup (125 mL) crumbled cooked ground beef

½ cup (125 mL) shredded Cheddar cheese

¼ cup (60 mL) salsa

Sour cream, chopped green onions and diced tomatoes (optional)

1 In the mug, combine potatoes, ground beef, cheese and salsa. Stir well.

2 Microwave, uncovered, on High for 2½ to 3 minutes, or until heated through. Top with sour cream, chopped green onions and diced tomatoes (if using).

tip

Omit ground beef and substitute ½ cup (125 mL) canned kidney, pinto or black beans, drained and rinsed.

MAKE IT TO GO

Combine ingredients in the mug as directed in Step 1. Cover mug, close vent and pack with ice packs. Pack sour cream and diced tomatoes separately in sealed, travel-safe containers with ice packs. Pack green onion in a ziplock bag. When ready to eat, open vent and continue as directed in Step 2.

BEEF TACOS

Taco Tuesday is a great tradition, but any day can be a taco day. This family favorite is a guaranteed lunchbox winner.

MAKES 1 SERVING | 1 (20 oz/625 g) microwave mug with vented cover

½ cup (125 mL) crumbled cooked ground beef

2 tbsp (30 mL) salsa or taco sauce

1 tsp (5 mL) dry minced onion

1 tsp (5 mL) chili seasoning

¼ tsp (1 mL) salt

2 crisp taco shells

2 tbsp (30 mL) shredded Cheddar cheese

Salsa, shredded lettuce and chopped tomatoes (optional)

1 In the mug, combine beef, salsa, onion, chili seasoning and salt.

2 Microwave, covered, on High for 1 minute. Let stand, covered, for 1 minute.

3 Spoon meat into taco shells. Top with cheese and add salsa, lettuce and tomatoes (if using).

tips

Brown the ground beef the night before and refrigerate it overnight. In the morning you can quickly combine the chilled beef with the remaining ingredients.

If you prefer a soft-shell taco, substitute a flour tortilla for the crisp taco shells. Place tortilla in a paper towel and microwave for 10 seconds or until warm. Spoon the prepared meat mixture into tortilla and top as desired.

MAKE IT TO GO

Combine ingredients in the mug as directed in Step 1. Cover mug, close vent and pack with ice packs. Pack taco shells, cheese, salsa, shredded lettuce, chopped tomatoes or other favorite taco toppings in separate containers or ziplock bags with ice packs. When ready to eat, open vent and continue as directed in Step 2.

ENCHILADA STACK

We have memories of the entire kitchen being a mess when preparing traditional enchiladas in a baking pan, but not so with this recipe, which comes together in minutes and with no mess!

MAKES 1 SERVING | 1 (20 oz/625 g) microwave mug with vented cover

2 6-inch (15 cm) corn tortillas

1/2 cup (125 mL) red or green enchilada sauce

1/2 cup (125 mL) crumbled cooked ground beef

1/2 cup (125 mL) shredded Cheddar cheese

1 tbsp (15 mL) sour cream

1 tbsp (15 mL) chopped green onion

tip

Omit beef and substitute 1/2 cup (125 mL) canned red or pinto beans, drained and rinsed, for a vegetarian option.

variation

Crunchy Enchilada: Omit corn tortillas and substitute 1/2 cup (125 mL) crushed tortilla chips. Proceed as directed, using half of the crushed tortilla chips in place of each layer of corn tortillas. If you prefer a crunchy texture, do not make this variation to go.

1 Cut each tortilla into 6 equal-size wedges. Pour about 2 tbsp (30 mL) enchilada sauce in the mug. Layer 6 tortilla pieces over the sauce. Sprinkle with 1/4 cup (60 mL) ground beef and 3 tbsp (45 mL) cheese. Pour 3 tbsp (45 mL) enchilada sauce over the cheese. Top with remaining 6 pieces of tortillas. Sprinkle remaining beef over tortillas and sprinkle with 3 tbsp (45 mL) cheese. Pour 3 tbsp (45 mL) enchilada sauce over cheese. Sprinkle with remaining cheese.

2 Microwave, uncovered, on High for 2 1/2 minutes or until heated through. Dollop with sour cream and sprinkle with green onions.

MAKE IT TO GO

Combine ingredients in the mug as directed in Step 1. Cover mug, close vent and pack with ice packs. Pack sour cream and green onion in separate containers with ice packs. When ready to eat, uncover and continue as directed in Step 2.

FRITO PIE

Frito pie traditionally is not a pie at all but instead corn chips with a chili-type mixture on top. It is most often served straight from the corn chip bag, but this is a much easier to eat version. Texas and New Mexico both claim that this iconic meal originated in their state. No matter the origins, it is always topped with shredded cheese.

MAKES 1 SERVING | 1 (20 oz/625 g) microwave mug with vented cover

½ cup (125 mL) crumbled cooked ground beef

½ cup (125 mL) canned pinto or red beans, drained and rinsed

⅓ cup (75 mL) taco sauce or salsa

1 tsp (5 mL) dry minced onion

½ cup (125 mL) regular-size corn chips

2 tbsp (30 mL) shredded Cheddar cheese

1 tbsp (15 mL) sour cream

3 slices pickled jalapeños, drained (optional)

1 In the mug, stir together ground beef, beans, taco sauce and onion.

2 Microwave, covered, on High for 2 to 2½ minutes. Stir in corn chips and cheese. Dollop with sour cream and top with jalapeños (if using). Serve immediately.

MAKE IT TO GO

Combine ingredients in the mug as directed in Step 1. Cover mug, close vent and pack with ice packs. Place corn chips in a ziplock bag. Pack cheese, sour cream and jalapeños (if using) in separate containers with ice packs. When ready to eat, open vent and continue as directed in Step 2.

GINGER-GLAZED MEATBALLS

When you keep fully cooked meatballs in the freezer, you can enjoy a variety of meals with little to no plan-ahead time.

MAKES 1 SERVING | 1 (20 oz/625 g) microwave mug with vented cover

1 tbsp (15 mL) liquid honey

1 tbsp (15 mL) soy sauce

1 tbsp (15 mL) rice vinegar

2 tsp (10 mL) dark sesame oil

1 tsp (5 mL) grated gingerroot

1/2 tsp (2 mL) garlic chili sauce

6 to 8 frozen fully cooked appetizer meatballs, thawed

Finely chopped green onion, toasted sesame seeds and cooked white rice (optional)

tip

No time to thaw frozen appetizer meatballs? No problem. Increase microwave time in Step 2 to 4 minutes.

1 In the mug, combine honey, soy sauce, vinegar, sesame oil, ginger and chili sauce; stir to blend well. Place meatballs in mug and stir to coat with sauce.

2 Microwave, covered, on High for 2 to 2 1/2 minutes. Sprinkle with green onion and toasted sesame seeds (if using). Serve on cooked white rice (if using).

MAKE IT TO GO

Combine ingredients in the mug as directed in Step 1. Cover mug, close vent and pack with ice packs. Pack green onion, sesame seeds and rice in separate containers with ice packs. When ready to eat, open vent and continue as directed in Step 2. It may be more convenient to stir the rice into the meatballs and microwave, uncovered, for 30 seconds to 1 minutes to heat through. Sprinkle with green onion and toasted sesame seeds.

JAMBALAYA

Jambalaya is a famous New Orleans dish with influences from the recipes of Spain, France and Africa. Creole and Cajun cuisine originated in Louisiana and always has a base of onion, bell peppers and celery. With this base and seasoning you can also create other Louisiana-inspired recipes such as gumbo.

MAKES 1 SERVING | 1 (20 oz/625 g) microwave mug with vented cover

2 tbsp (30 mL) finely chopped onion

2 tbsp (30 mL) finely chopped celery

2 tbsp (30 mL) finely chopped green bell pepper

1 tsp (5 mL) olive oil

½ tsp (2 mL) Cajun or Creole seasoning

¼ tsp (1 mL) garlic powder

¼ (1 mL) tsp salt

¾ cup (175 mL) cooked white rice

½ cup (125 mL) diced smoked turkey sausage

½ cup (125 mL) chopped cooked chicken

⅔ cup (150 mL) canned diced tomatoes with juice

1 tsp (5 mL) Worcestershire sauce

Hot pepper sauce (optional)

1 In the mug, combine onion, celery, green pepper, oil, Cajun seasoning, garlic powder and salt.

2 Microwave, covered, on High for 1½ minutes. Stir in rice, smoked sausage, chicken, diced tomatoes and Worcestershire sauce. Microwave, covered on High for 2½ to 3 minutes. Serve with hot pepper sauce (if using).

MAKE IT TO GO

Combine ingredients in the mug as directed in Step 1. Cover mug, close vent and pack with ice packs. Pack rice, smoked sausage, chicken, tomatoes and Worcestershire sauce in a separate container with ice packs. When ready to eat, open vent and continue as directed in Step 2.

tip

The chicken can be omitted and coarsely chopped cooked shrimp can be substituted. Stir shrimp in after cooking is complete and season with hot pepper sauce.

SALSA CHICKEN AND PEPPERS

This recipe can be adapted to fit your mood and served in a variety of ways. Try it straight from the mug for a delicious meal, served with cooked rice for a filling variation or, our favorite, tucked into a flour tortilla for a simple type of chicken fajita. Goodbye, ho-hum lunches and dinners!

MAKES 1 SERVING | 1 (20 oz/625 g) microwave mug with vented cover

1 cup (250 mL) thinly sliced red, green or yellow bell peppers (cut into strips)

¼ cup (60 mL) thinly sliced onion

2 tsp (10 mL) olive oil

½ tsp (2 mL) ground cumin

¼ tsp (1 mL) chili powder

Salt and ground black pepper

½ cup (125 mL) chopped cooked chicken

⅓ cup (75 mL) salsa

Cooked rice or flour tortilla (optional)

1 In the mug, combine peppers, onions, oil, cumin and chili powder. Season to taste with salt and pepper.

2 Microwave, uncovered, on High for 1½ minutes or until vegetables are tender.

3 Stir in chicken and salsa. Microwave, uncovered, on High for 1½ minutes. Serve immediately. If desired, spoon over rice or, using a slotted spoon, tuck into a flour tortilla (if using).

tip

Leftover steak strips can be substituted for the chicken to create Salsa Beef and Peppers.

MAKE IT TO GO

Combine ingredients in the mug as directed in Step 1. Cover mug, close vent and pack with ice packs. Pack chicken and salsa in a separate container with ice packs. Pack rice or tortilla (if using) in a separate container or ziplock bag. When ready to eat, open vent and continue as directed in Step 2.

EASY CHICKEN LO MEIN

The delicious aroma of Lo Mein, a soft noodle dish, wafts from our local Chinese restaurants. This quick mug recipe is inspired by that dish and features chicken, vegetables and noodles.

MAKES 1 SERVING | 1 (20 oz/625 g) microwave mug with vented cover

¾ cup (175 mL) frozen Asian vegetable blend or stir-fry blend

½ cup (125 mL) chopped cooked chicken

2 tbsp (30 mL) very finely chopped carrots

1 tbsp (15 mL) hoisin sauce

1 tbsp (15 mL) soy sauce

1 tbsp (15 mL) water

1 cup (250 mL) cooked Asian lo mein noodles or linguini

½ tsp (2 mL) sesame oil

1 In the mug, combine vegetables, chicken, carrots, hoisin sauce, soy sauce and water.

2 Microwave, covered, on High for 3 minutes. Stir in the noodles and sesame oil. Continue to microwave, covered, for 30 seconds. Let rest 1 minute.

MAKE IT TO GO

Combine ingredients in the mug as directed in Step 1. Cover mug, close vent and pack with ice packs. Place the noodles and the sesame oil together in a container or ziplock bag. When ready to eat, open vent and continue as directed in Step 2. If the vegetables are thawed, reduce cooking time to 2 minutes.

tips

Asian or stir-fry vegetable blends are readily available frozen and feature a variety of flavors. Some may include green beans, broccoli, onions and mushrooms, while another brand may incorporate sliced bell peppers or carrots. Choose the flavor you enjoy most.

What is hoisin sauce? Look for bottles of this sweet and spicy sauce shelved with Asian foods at the grocery store.

CHICKEN LETTUCE WRAP

A quick lunch never tasted so good! Lettuce wraps are a signature appetizer or entrée item on many restaurant menus. This light and healthy version features chicken and vegetables and couldn't be easier to make.

MAKES 1 SERVING | 1 (20 oz/625 g) microwave mug with vented cover

¾ cup (175 mL) crumbled cooked ground chicken

2 tbsp (30 mL) chopped canned water chestnuts, drained, or chopped celery

2 tbsp (30 mL) finely chopped green onions

1 tbsp (15 mL) hoisin sauce

½ tsp (2 mL) garlic powder

⅛ tsp (0.5 mL) hot pepper sauce, such as Siracha, or to taste

4 to 5 butter lettuce leaves

Soy sauce, for serving (optional)

1 In the mug, combine chicken, water chestnuts, green onions, hoisin sauce, garlic powder and hot pepper sauce.

2 Microwave, covered, on High for 1½ minutes. Let rest 1 minute.

3 To serve, spoon the chicken mixture onto a lettuce leaf. Drizzle with soy sauce (if using). Gently fold the lettuce leaf over the filling.

MAKE IT TO GO

Combine ingredients in the mug as directed in Step 1. Cover mug, close vent and pack with ice packs. Pack lettuce leaves in a damp paper towel in a ziplock bag with ice packs. Pack extra soy sauce in a small, sealed travel-safe container. When ready to eat, open vent and continue as directed in Step 2.

tips

Water chestnuts add a delicious, crunchy taste to any salad or casserole. Store leftover water chestnuts with the liquid from the can, covered, in the refrigerator and use within one week.

While the flavor will be different, chopped celery could be substituted for the water chestnuts and will provide a crunchy texture.

EGG ROLL IN A MUG

Egg rolls are savored for their crunchy, fried exterior and hot filling of meat and vegetables. We captured those same sensations in this easy mug recipe by topping the mug of hot chicken and vegetables with crisp, wonton strips for added flavor and texture.

MAKES 1 SERVING | 1 (20 oz/625 g) microwave mug with vented cover

1 cup (250 mL) coleslaw mix

½ cup (125 mL) crumbled cooked ground chicken

1 tbsp (15 mL) finely chopped green onions

2 tsp (10 mL) soy sauce

2 tsp (10 mL) water

1 tsp (5 mL) rice vinegar

¼ tsp (1 mL) garlic powder

¼ tsp (1 mL) ground ginger

Crisp wonton strips

1 In the mug, combine coleslaw, chicken, green onions, soy sauce, water, vinegar, garlic powder and ginger.

2 Microwave, covered, on High for 3 minutes. Let rest 1 minute.

3 Top with crisp wonton strips.

MAKE IT TO GO

Combine ingredients in the mug as directed in Step 1. Cover mug, close vent and pack with ice packs. Pack crisp wonton strips in a separate container or ziplock bag. When ready to eat, open vent and continue as directed in Step 2.

tip

Crisp wonton strips are an easy way to add crunchy flavor to this mug meal recipe or any of your favorite soups or salads. Look for them in bags shelved near the croutons or other salad toppings.

CHEESY CHICKEN ENCHILADA WITH REFRIED BEANS

No more racing through the fast-food drive-through for Mexican-inspired meals. This chicken enchilada will be out of the microwave in minutes, leaving plenty of time for a leisurely lunch.

MAKES 1 SERVING | 1 (20 oz/625 g) microwave mug with vented cover

¼ cup (60 mL) refried beans

1 corn tortilla

½ cup (125 mL) chopped cooked chicken

3 tbsp (45 mL) shredded Cheddar cheese

¼ cup (60 mL) red enchilada sauce

1 tbsp (15 mL) sour cream

1 tbsp (15 mL) chopped green onion

1 Spread refried beans on one side of the corn tortilla. Nestle the tortilla, bean-side up, in the bottom of the mug and top with chicken and cheese. Pour enchilada sauce evenly over cheese.

2 Microwave, uncovered, on High for 2 to 2½ minutes or until heated through. Dollop with sour cream and chopped green onion.

tip

Store extra refried beans by removing from the can and placing into a freezer-safe container. Store in freezer for up to 6 months. When ready to use, place in refrigerator to thaw overnight.

MAKE IT TO GO

Combine ingredients in the mug as directed in Step 1, except do not pour the enchilada sauce over the cheese. Cover mug, close vent and pack with ice packs. Pack enchilada sauce, sour cream and green onions in separate containers with ice packs. When ready to eat, pour enchilada sauce over cheese and continue as directed in Step 2.

QUICK CHICKEN CHOW MEIN

Chow mein is a popular dish served throughout the world. While it originated in China, the recipe is often adapted to local preferences. No, you cannot stir-fry in your mug, but you can add a little crunch to this quick meal with crisp chow mein noodles, available packaged and ready to use.

MAKES 1 SERVING | 1 (20 oz/625 g) microwave mug with vented cover

¾ cup (175 mL) coleslaw mix

½ cup (125 mL) chopped cooked chicken

⅓ cup (75 mL) bean sprouts

2 tbsp (30 mL) chopped celery

1 tbsp (15 mL) finely chopped onion

2 tbsp (30 mL) soy sauce

1½ tbsp (22 mL) water

½ tsp (2 mL) packed dark brown sugar

⅛ tsp (0.5 mL) ground ginger

Ground black pepper

¼ cup (60 mL) crisp chow mein noodles

1 In the mug, combine coleslaw, chicken, bean sprouts, celery and onion. In a small bowl, combine soy sauce, water, brown sugar and ginger. Pour sauce over chicken and vegetables. Season to taste with pepper.

2 Microwave, covered, on High for 3 minutes. Top with chow mein noodles.

MAKE IT TO GO

Combine ingredients in the mug as directed in Step 1. Cover mug, close vent and pack with ice packs. Pack chow mein noodles in a ziplock bag. When ready to eat, open vent and continue as directed in Step 2.

tip

For additional flavor, add 1 tbsp (15 mL) bottled oyster sauce along with the soy sauce and water.

BUFFALO CHICKEN WITH CAULIFLOWER

Those famous Buffalo wings are the inspiration for this delicious recipe. Expecting hot and spicy chicken wings with a side of celery and maybe a blue cheese dip? Those flavors are all here in this easy-to-prepare mug meal.

MAKES 1 SERVING | 1 (20 oz/625 g) microwave mug with vented cover

1 cup (250 mL) finely chopped cauliflower

½ cup (125 mL) chopped cooked chicken

¼ cup (60 mL) finely chopped celery

2 tbsp (30 mL) Buffalo wing sauce

2 tbsp (30 mL) ranch dressing

Salt and ground black pepper

2 tbsp (30 mL) grated Parmesan cheese

Blue cheese crumbles (optional)

1 In the mug, combine cauliflower, chicken and celery. Stir in wing sauce and ranch dressing. Season to taste with salt and pepper.

2 Microwave, covered, on High for 3 minutes. Stir in Parmesan cheese. Cover and let stand for 1 minute. Sprinkle with blue cheese (if using).

MAKE IT TO GO

Combine ingredients in the mug as directed in Step 1. Cover mug, close vent and pack with ice packs. Pack Parmesan cheese and blue cheese (if using) in separate containers or ziplock bags with ice packs. When ready to eat, open vent and continue as directed in Step 2.

tip

If you want to make your Buffalo Chicken with Cauliflower milder, increase ranch dressing to 3 tbsp (45 mL) and reduce wing sauce to 1 tbsp (15 mL). For more spice, increase wing sauce to 3 tbsp (45 mL) and reduce ranch dressing to 1 tbsp (15 mL).

CHICKEN WITH TOMATOES, OREGANO AND PITA

This easy, delicious recipe can be quickly prepared whenever hunger strikes. Warm, cheesy chicken, seasoned with oregano and tomatoes, ideal for either lunch or dinner, provides a relaxing, nourishing break on a busy day.

MAKES 1 SERVING | 1 (20 oz/625 g) microwave mug with vented cover

½ cup (125 mL) chopped cooked chicken

¼ cup (60 mL) canned diced tomatoes with juice

¼ cup (60 mL) chopped red onion

2 tbsp (30 mL) chopped roasted red pepper, drained (see tip)

2 tbsp (30 mL) Italian salad dressing

¼ tsp (1 mL) dried oregano

Salt and ground black pepper

⅓ cup (75 mL) shredded Italian blend or mozzarella cheese

1 pita bread or crisp pita chips (optional)

1 In the mug, combine chicken, tomatoes, onion, red pepper, Italian dressing and oregano. Season to taste with salt and pepper.

2 Microwave, covered, on High for 2 to 2½ minutes. Top with cheese. Cover and let stand 1 minute.

3 Spoon onto pita bread or serve accompanied with pita chips (if using).

MAKE IT TO GO

Combine ingredients in the mug as directed in Step 1. Cover mug, close vent and pack with ice packs. Pack pita bread or chips (if using) in a ziplock bag. When ready to eat, open vent and continue as directed in Step 2.

tip

Roasted red peppers, readily available in jars at the grocery store, add color and flavor to your recipes with little effort. Once opened, store in the refrigerator and use within about a week.

HOT CHICKEN SALAD

Warm chicken salad is delicious yet comforting. For an added flavor pop, stir in dried sweetened cranberries or a chopped green onion. Serve with crackers or spoon into a pita pocket bread.

MAKES 1 SERVING | 1 (20 oz/625 g) microwave mug with vented cover

1 cup (250 mL) chopped cooked chicken

1/3 cup (75 mL) shredded Cheddar cheese

1 celery stalk, chopped

2 tbsp (30 mL) slivered almonds

1/3 cup (75 mL) mayonnaise

Salt and ground black pepper

Crackers (optional)

1 In the mug, combine chicken, cheese, celery and almonds. Stir in mayonnaise. Season to taste with salt and pepper.

2 Microwave, covered, on High for 2 minutes. Let rest 1 minute. Serve with crackers (if using).

tip

If desired, add 2 tbsp (30 mL) dried, sweetened cranberries or 1 tbsp (15 mL) finely chopped green onion to the salad in Step 1.

MAKE IT TO GO

Combine ingredients in the mug as directed in Step 1. Cover mug, close vent and pack with ice packs. Pack crackers (if using) in a ziplock bag. When ready to eat, open vent and continue as directed in Step 2.

KENTUCKY HOT BROWN TURKEY MUG

The Kentucky Hot Brown is a classic, open-faced turkey sandwich that originated at the Brown Hotel in Louisville, Kentucky. This mug recipe is inspired by that delicious sandwich.

MAKES 1 SERVING | 1 (20 oz/625 g) microwave mug with vented cover

2 deli slices roasted turkey, cut into quarters

1 slice cooked bacon, cut into thirds

1 slice Cheddar cheese, cut into quarters

3 tbsp (45 mL) cream cheese, softened

2 tbsp (30 mL) milk

1 to 2 drops hot pepper sauce (optional)

2 tbsp (30 mL) grated Parmesan cheese

1 slice thick white bread or Texas toast, toasted

1 to 2 slices tomato

Minced fresh chives (optional)

1 In the mug, stack turkey, bacon and cheese.

2 In a small bowl, combine cream cheese, milk and hot sauce (if using). Stir in Parmesan cheese. Spoon mixture over Cheddar cheese in the mug.

3 Microwave, uncovered, on High for 1 minute, or until hot and the cheese is melted.

4 Place toast on a serving plate. Spoon hot turkey, bacon and cheese mixture over toast. Top with tomato. Stir together any cheese sauce remaining in the mug, then spoon over tomato. Sprinkle with chives (if using).

tips

On toast is the classic way to serve this sandwich, but the warm turkey and cheese is tasty served with any bread or cracker.

For best results, use bacon that is fully cooked but not crisp, as the bacon will cook more in the microwave oven.

MAKE IT TO GO

Prepare recipe through Step 2. Cover mug, close vent and pack with ice packs. Place bread in a ziplock bag. Sprinkle tomato slice with chives (if using) and pack in a separate container or ziplock bag. When ready to eat, uncover and continue as directed in Step 3.

snacks and desserts

GARLIC WHITE BEAN SNACK SPREAD

White bean spread is a classic simple and healthy spread for crostini. Crostini are small pieces of toast, easily made by toasting thin slices of baguette. Packaged crostini are now available at many stores, or you could substitute crackers. No matter what you spread it on, this recipe is super easy to make and a perfect afternoon snack or appetizer with a glass of wine.

MAKES 1 TO 2 SERVINGS |
1 (20 oz/625 g) microwave mug with vented cover

¾ cup (175 mL) canned cannellini beans, drained and rinsed

1 tbsp (15 mL) ready-to-use vegetable or chicken broth or water

1 tbsp (15 mL) freshly squeezed lemon juice

2 tsp (10 mL) olive oil

⅛ tsp (0.5 mL) garlic powder

Salt and ground black pepper

Fresh minced parsley, rosemary leaves or dill weed (optional)

Crostini or crackers

1 In the mug, combine beans, broth, lemon juice, oil and garlic powder. Season to taste with salt and pepper.

2 Microwave, covered, on High for 1 minute. Using the back of a fork, mash beans until desired consistency is reached, making it as smooth or as chunky as you prefer.

3 Sprinkle with parsley (if using). Serve as a spread on crostini or crackers.

tips

The spread is best served warm and freshly made.

Cannellini beans are an Italian white kidney bean and are readily available canned. They are more tender than Great Northern beans, but in a pinch, you can substitute Great Northern beans.

MAKE IT TO GO

Combine ingredients in the mug as directed in Step 1. Cover mug, close vent and pack with ice packs. Pack parsley (if using) and crostini or crackers separately in ziplock bags. When ready to eat, open vent and continue as directed in Step 2.

HOT PIZZA DIP

You won't have to order pizza delivery on those late nights when you are craving that hot, cheesy goodness. Delicious pizza flavors are ready in just moments.

MAKES 2 SERVINGS | 1 (20 oz/625 g) microwave mug with vented cover

½ cup (125 mL) pizza sauce

3 tbsp (45 mL) garlic and herb cream cheese or plain cream cheese

½ tsp (2 mL) dried oregano leaves

6 tbsp (90 mL) shredded mozzarella cheese, divided

1 tbsp (15 mL) grated Parmesan cheese

1 tbsp (15 mL) finely diced green pepper, chopped ripe olives or chopped pepperoni (optional)

Crisp bread sticks or pita chips

1 In the mug, stir together pizza sauce, cream cheese and oregano. Stir in ¼ cup (60 mL) mozzarella and the Parmesan.

2 Microwave, covered, on High for 1 minute. Stir. Top with remaining 2 tbsp (30 mL) mozzarella and green pepper (if using). Continue to microwave, covered, on High for 30 seconds. Let stand, covered, for 1 minute. Serve with bread sticks or pita chips.

MAKE IT TO GO

Combine ingredients in the mug as directed in Step 1. Cover mug, close vent and pack with ice packs. Pack remaining cheese, green pepper and bread sticks in separate containers or ziplock bags with ice packs. When ready to eat, open vent and continue as directed in Step 2.

HERBED PRETZELS

Tired of plain pretzels when the afternoon rolls around and you need a pick-me-up? In a matter of minutes, you can solve the problem and add zip to your pretzels.

MAKES 1 SERVING | 1 (20 oz/625 g) microwave mug with vented cover

1½ tbsp (22 mL) butter, cut into small cubes

½ tsp (2 mL) dried parsley flakes

¼ tsp (1 mL) lemon pepper

¼ tsp (1 mL) garlic powder

¼ tsp (1 mL) dried dillweed

1½ cups (375 mL) mini pretzel bites

tip

Stick pretzels can be broken in two and used in place of the mini pretzel bites.

1 In the mug, place butter. Microwave, uncovered, on High for 30 seconds. Stir in parsley, lemon pepper, garlic powder and dillweed.

2 Add pretzels and stir to coat. Microwave, uncovered, on High for 1 minute. Stir and continue to microwave, uncovered, on High for 30 seconds. Allow to cool for at least 10 minutes.

MAKE IT TO GO

Place butter and seasonings in the mug as directed in Step 1, but do not microwave. Cover mug, close vent and pack. Pack pretzels in a ziplock bag. When ready to eat, uncover mug and microwave on High for 30 seconds. Stir and continue as directed in Step 2.

CRUNCH MIX

Crunch mix, snack mix, munch mix — call it whatever you like. This is addictive in a good way after a busy day at the office or when the midnight oil burns as you prepare to take a final exam. Come to think of it, we enjoy this snack anytime, day or night, and have even been known to call this breakfast.

MAKES 1 SERVING | 1 (20 oz/625 g) microwave mug with vented cover

½ cup (125 mL) O-shaped cereal

¼ cup (60 mL) pretzel bites

¼ cup (60 mL) wheat square cereal

¼ cup (60 mL) rice square cereal

¼ cup (60 mL) corn square cereal

2 tbsp (30 mL) nuts (see tip)

1½ tbsp (22 mL) butter, cut into small cubes

1½ tsp (7 mL) Worcestershire sauce

¼ tsp (1 mL) seasoned salt

¼ tsp (1 mL) garlic powder

1 Place the cereals, pretzels and nuts in a ziplock bag. Set aside.

2 In the mug, combine butter, Worcestershire sauce, seasoned salt and garlic powder.

3 Microwave, uncovered, on High for 30 seconds or until butter is melted. Stir well. Pour butter mixture over cereal and gently toss to blend and coat. Pour the cereal into the mug.

4 Microwave, uncovered, on High for 1½ minutes. Stir and continue to microwave, uncovered, on High for 45 seconds. Allow to cool for at least 10 minutes before enjoying.

tips

Substitute your favorite cereal pieces for any of the cereals listed.

Use your favorite variety of nut in this recipe. We like to include pecan halves, almonds, cashews or peanuts.

MAKE IT TO GO

Pack cereals, pretzels and nuts together in a ziplock bag as directed in Step 1. Combine ingredients in the mug as directed in Step 2. Cover mug, close vent and pack. When ready to eat, open vent and continue as directed in Step 3.

GRANOLA AND FRUIT CRISP

The name of this granola says it all, for it is crisp, even though it is cooked in the microwave oven. It makes the perfect snack anytime you crave a crunchy sweet treat. Customize the flavor by using your favorite variety of nut or dried fruit.

MAKES 1 SERVING | 1 (20 oz/625 g) microwave mug with vented cover

⅔ cup (150 mL) large-flake (old-fashioned) rolled oats

¼ (60 mL) chopped walnuts

1 tbsp (15 mL) butter, cut in small cubes

1 tbsp (15 mL) liquid honey

2 tsp (10 mL) packed dark brown sugar

¼ tsp (1 mL) ground cinnamon

¼ cup (60 mL) raisins

1 In the mug, combine oats, walnuts, butter, honey, brown sugar and cinnamon.

2 Microwave, uncovered, on High for 30 seconds. Stir and continue to microwave, uncovered, on High for 1 minute.

3 Stir in raisins. Line a plate with parchment paper or waxed paper. Carefully pour hot granola mixture onto the prepared plate and, using a spoon, spread until granola is in a single even layer. Let cool completely.

variation

Tropical Granola and Fruit Crisp: Substitute whole almonds for the walnuts and chopped dried pineapple or mango for the raisins. Stir in 2 tbsp (30 mL) sweetened, flaked coconut along with fruit. Proceed as recipe directs.

MAKE IT TO GO

Combine ingredients in the mug as directed in Step 1. Cover mug, close vent and pack. Pack raisins in a separate ziplock bag. Remember to pack a sheet of parchment paper or waxed paper to use for lining a plate. When ready to eat, uncover and continue as directed in Step 2.

BLUEBERRY CRUMBLE

It is rare that a sweet treat is also packed with nutrition, but that is the case for this recipe. Blueberries are a powerhouse of nutrition. Here, they are sweetened with just a hint of sugar, then topped with the goodness of a crunchy oat granola bar and almonds.

MAKES 1 SERVING | 1 (20 oz/625 g) microwave mug with vented cover

¾ cup (175 mL) fresh or frozen blueberries

1 tbsp (15 mL) granulated sugar

½ tsp (2 mL) cornstarch

1 packet (1.49 oz/42 g) crunchy oat granola bars, chopped

2 tbsp (30 mL) sliced almonds

1 tbsp (15 mL) butter, melted

1 In the mug, combine blueberries, sugar and cornstarch.

2 In a small bowl, stir together chopped granola bar, almonds and butter. Spoon granola mixture over blueberries.

3 Microwave, uncovered, on High for 1½ to 2 minutes or until blueberries are hot and beginning to bubble. Let stand for 3 minutes.

tip

Substitute ⅔ cup (150 mL) low-fat granola for the chopped granola bar.

MAKE IT TO GO

Combine ingredients in the mug as directed in Step 1. Cover mug, close vent and pack with ice packs. Toss chopped granola bar and almonds with the melted butter and pack in a sealed container or ziplock bag. When ready to eat, spoon granola mixture over blueberries, and continue as directed in Step 3.

CHERRY CRISP

You can enjoy a delicious cherry crisp and not deal with a large pan of leftovers. Enjoy this warm and, better yet, add a scoop of ice cream on top.

MAKES 1 SERVING | 1 (20 oz/625 g) microwave mug with vented cover

1 cup (250 mL) fresh or frozen, pitted, sweet cherries

1½ tbsp (22 mL) granulated sugar

½ tsp (2 mL) almond extract

¼ cup (60 mL) all-purpose flour

1½ tbsp (22 mL) packed dark brown sugar

½ tsp (2 mL) baking powder

1 tbsp (15 mL) chopped pecans

1 tbsp (15 mL) large-flake (old-fashioned) rolled oats

3 tbsp (45 mL) milk

1½ tbsp (22 mL) butter, cut into thin slivers

1 In the mug, combine cherries, sugar and almond extract.

2 In a small bowl, combine flour, brown sugar, baking powder, pecans and oats. Stir in milk until blended well.

3 Dollop batter on top of the cherries. Cover evenly with slivers of butter. Microwave, covered, on High for 2 to 2½ minutes.

tip

Substitute another fruit for the cherries.

MAKE IT TO GO

Combine ingredients in the mug as directed in Step 1. Cover mug, close vent and pack with ice packs. Combine flour, brown sugar, baking powder, pecans and oats in a separate container. Stir in milk until smooth. Seal and place with ice packs. Pack butter in a ziplock bag with ice pack. When ready to eat, open vent and continue as directed in Step 3.

CHOCOLATE PEANUT BUTTER CRUNCH

Who doesn't need a pick-me-up after a full day of classes or meetings? It takes only minutes to stir together this crunchy chocolate treat. Think of it as a sweet reward for all your hard work.

**MAKES 1 TO 2 SERVINGS |
1 (20 oz/625 g) microwave mug with vented cover**

3 oz (90 g) chocolate-flavored almond bark, finely chopped

2 tbsp (30 mL) peanut butter

¾ cup (175 mL) crisp rice cereal

tip

If you can't wait an hour or two for the Chocolate Peanut Butter Crunch to set, it is still yummy. Just grab a spoon and enjoy the warm chocolate sweet treat.

1 In the mug, place chocolate. Microwave, uncovered, on High for 1 minute. Stir in peanut butter. Continue to microwave, uncovered, on High for 30 to 45 seconds or until chocolate is melted. Stir until smooth.

2 Add crisp rice cereal and stir to coat. Pat mixture evenly in the mug. Allow to stand for an hour or two until firm and set.

3 Carefully run a knife around the inside edge of the mug. Cut the crunch into quarters and using a metal spatula, remove from the mug. Enjoy!

MAKE IT TO GO

Prepare the recipe as directed, through to and including adding the crisp rice cereal in Step 2. Cover mug, close vent and pack. When ready to eat, uncover and cut into pieces as directed in Step 3.

CANDY-STUDDED MARSHMALLOW TREATS

Kids love crispy marshmallow treats and, truth be known, adults love them just as much. The beauty of this recipe is that it makes just enough to enjoy without leftovers.

**MAKES 1 TO 2 SERVINGS |
1 (20 oz/625 g) microwave mug with vented cover**

Nonstick cooking spray

2 tbsp (30 mL) unsalted butter, cut into cubes

1⅓ cups (325 mL) mini marshmallows

1 cup (250 mL) crisp cereal

3 tbsp (45 mL) candy-coated chocolate pieces

tip

Omit the candy-coated pieces and add 3 tbsp (45 mL) roasted peanuts.

1 Spray the mug with nonstick cooking spray. Place butter cubes into the mug. Add mini marshmallows on top.

2 Microwave, uncovered, on High for 30 seconds. Stir well. Add crisp cereal and stir to coat. Fold in candy pieces. Allow to stand until firm or enjoy warm with a spoon.

MAKE IT TO GO

Combine ingredients in the mug as directed in Step 1. Cover mug, close vent and pack with ice packs. Pack cereal and candy in separate containers or ziplock bags. When ready to eat, open vent and continue as directed in Step 2.

CINNAMON-TOASTED PECANS

Pecans, always a favorite snack, are elevated to a new level with the addition of sugar and cinnamon. Keep these in the freezer and pull them out to top salads for an extra pop of flavor.

MAKES 1 SERVING | 1 (20 oz/625 g) microwave mug with vented cover

1 tbsp (15 mL) butter, cut into small cubes

1 cup (250 mL) pecan halves

¼ cup (60 mL) sugar

½ tsp (2 mL) ground cinnamon

---

tip

If you enjoy the flavor of nutmeg, add ¼ tsp (1 mL) along with the cinnamon.

1 Place butter in the mug.

2 Microwave, uncovered, on High for 30 to 40 seconds until butter is melted.

3 Place pecan halves in plastic bag. Drizzle melted butter over pecans. Pour sugar and cinnamon over pecans. Toss bag to coat evenly. Pour pecans into the mug. Microwave, uncovered, on Medium-High (70%) power for 2 minutes, stirring halfway through. Let cool for 10 to 15 minutes. For quicker cooling, spread pecans on a plate.

MAKE IT TO GO

Place butter in the mug as directed in Step 1. Cover mug, close vent and pack. Pack pecan halves in a ziplock bag and sugar and cinnamon in a separate ziplock bag. When ready to eat, uncover and continue as directed in Step 2.

HOT COCOA

This cocoa has a deep, rich flavor that satisfies any day, no matter what the weather. Treat yourself to a chocolate beverage when you need a personal pick-me-up.

MAKES 1 SERVING | 1 (20 oz/625 g) microwave mug with vented cover

2 tbsp (30 mL) granulated sugar

2 tbsp (30 mL) unsweetened cocoa powder

1 tbsp (15 mL) water

Pinch of salt

1 cup (250 mL) milk

¼ tsp (1 mL) vanilla extract

2 tbsp (30 mL) miniature marshmallows

1 In the mug, combine sugar, cocoa, water and salt.

2 Microwave, uncovered, on High for 45 seconds. Stir in milk until blended. Microwave, uncovered, on High for 1½ to 2 minutes. Stir in vanilla and top with marshmallows.

MAKE IT TO GO

Combine ingredients in the mug as directed in Step 1. Cover mug, close vent and pack. Pack milk in a sealed, travel-safe container with ice packs. Pack vanilla and marshmallows in separate containers. When ready to drink, uncover and continue as directed in Step 2.

HOT SPICED CITRUS CIDER

This delightful hot drink makes a tasty change of pace from traditional spiced cider. We enjoy the fresh citrus taste, perfectly spiced with cinnamon, cloves and nutmeg, yet not too sweet.

MAKES 1 SERVING | 1 (20 oz/625 g) microwave mug with vented cover

1 cup (250 mL) apple cider

½ cup (125 mL) orange juice

2 tsp (10 mL) granulated sugar

2 whole cloves

1 3-inch (7.5 cm) cinnamon stick

Dash ground nutmeg

1 In the mug, combine cider, orange juice and sugar. Add cloves, cinnamon and nutmeg.

2 Microwave, uncovered, on High for 2 minutes. Stir well. Let rest 1 minute to steep. Remove cloves and cinnamon stick before serving.

MAKE IT TO GO

Combine ingredients in the mug as directed in Step 1. Cover mug, close vent and pack with ice packs. When ready to drink, uncover and proceed as recipe directs in Step 2.

Library and Archives Canada Cataloguing in Publication

Title: The official CorningWare Meal Mug cookbook : 75 easy microwave meals in minutes / Roxanne Wyss & Kathy Moore.

Other titles: 75 easy microwave meals in minutes | Seventy-five easy microwave meals in minutes

Names: Wyss, Roxanne, author. | Moore, Kathy, author.

Description: Includes index.

Identifiers: Canadiana 20210284056 | ISBN 9780778807056 (softcover)

Subjects: LCSH: Microwave cooking. | LCSH: Quick and easy cooking. | LCGFT: Cookbooks.

Classification: LCC TX832 .W97 2022 | DDC 641.5/882—dc23

index

honey
   Ginger-Glazed Meatballs, 121
   Granola and Fruit Crisp, 154
Hot Chicken Salad, 141
Hot Cocoa, 166
Hot Pizza Dip, 149
Hot Spiced Citrus Cider, 169

J

Jambalaya, 122

K

Kentucky Hot Brown Turkey Mug, 142
ketchup. *See* tomato sauces

maple syrup
   Berry French Toast, 20
   Maple Muesli with Apples and Pecans, 23
Marinara Meatball Soup, 29
marshmallows
   Candy-Studded Marshmallow Treats, 162
   Hot Cocoa, 166
mayonnaise (as ingredient)
   Hot Chicken Salad, 141
   Mexican-Style Street Corn, 92
meatballs
   Ginger-Glazed Meatballs, 121
   Marinara Meatball Soup, 29
   Spaghetti and Meatballs, 72
Mediterranean-Inspired Quinoa, Tomato and Feta, 104
Mexican-Style Street Corn, 92
milk and cream. *See also* sour cream
   Biscuit with Sausage Gravy, 19
   Broccoli Cheese Soup, 41
   Cheesy Rotini with Ham and Peas, 79
   Country Potato Soup, 42
   Cranberry Pecan Oatmeal, 24
   Crustless Quiche, 15
   Hot Cocoa, 166
   Maple Muesli with Apples and Pecans, 23
mug meals, 6–7

Mug Pad Thai, 87
Mushrooms and Spinach, Risotto with, 100

noodles. *See also* pasta
   Brown Rice Noodles with Vegetables, 84
   Easy Chicken Lo Mein, 126
   Mug Pad Thai, 87
   Quick Chicken Chow Mein, 134
   Ramen Mug, 88
nuts. *See also* seeds; *specific types of nuts*
   Crunch Mix, 153
   Granola and Fruit Crisp, 154

oats
   Cherry Crisp, 158
   Cranberry Pecan Oatmeal, 24
   Granola and Fruit Crisp, 154
   Maple Muesli with Apples and Pecans, 23
onions. *See also* onions, green
   Chicken with Tomatoes, Oregano and Pita, 138
   Mediterranean-Inspired Quinoa, Tomato and Feta, 104
   Salsa Chicken and Peppers, 125
   Salsa Rice Bowl, 99
onions, green
   Cheesy Chicken Enchilada with Refried Beans, 133
   Chicken Lettuce Wrap, 129
   Egg Roll in a Mug, 130
   Enchilada Stack, 117
   Fried Rice, 96
   Ginger Chicken Soup with Cabbage and Wontons, 38
   Hot Chicken Salad (tip), 141

pasta. *See also* noodles
   Cheeseburger Pasta, 76
   Cheesy Ravioli, 71
   Cheesy Rotini with Ham and Peas, 79
   Chili Mac, 68

T

V

W